Praise for CULTURE EATS STRATEGY

"Culture is the most often overlooked source of competitive advantage. Curt Coffman and Kathie Sorensen's cutting edge research defines what constitutes a winning culture, and provides a powerful prescription for creating and sustaining it."

-Kenneth W. Freeman, Allen Questrom Professor and Dean, Boston University School of Management and former Chairman and CEO of Quest Diagnostics

"Culture is probably the least understood element when an Organization undergoes a "Change Management" program. This book clearly explains why it should be the best understood element and offers very practical and pragmatic advice to help you get there. The anecdotes and stories etc. provide very relatable and recognizable examples that enable you to steer Leadership teams in the right direction. A quick but thorough read backed up with supportive data that makes the case for why understanding the culture leads to a highly engaged workforce."

-George Borst, President and CEO, Toyota Financial Services

In this well-written, common sense book, Coffman & Sorensen demystify how to build a high performance culture. Filled with practical suggestions about what to do and how to do it as well as diagnostic questions to help you think ough the process, *Culture* shows to unlock the vast, untapped human potential in all organizations

-Jeffrey Pfe er, Professor, Graduate School of Business, Stanford University and co-author of The Knowing-Doing Gap

"The importance of one's corporate culture to the lifeblood of a company is undeniable, yet so evasive: What is that magical spark to ignite your employee's passions in the office and create a truly magical place to work? Culture Eats Strategy for Lunch goes a long way towards answering those questions and unlocking the true passions and potential of your workforce."

-Jim Miller. VP of World Wide Operations, Google

Culture Eats Strategy for Lunch outlines a practical call to action that reminds us when it comes to culture, there are no spectators. Every individual has a role to play in the care and feeding of a workplace that invites a sense of belonging. This is really a story about creating a differentiated experience.

–Robb Webb, Chief Human Resource Officer, Hyatt Hotels Corporation

"Culture is a conversation, led by leaders, about what the company values and 'how things are done around here.' In this remarkable book, Curt & Kathie will show you how to shape, leap and refine the conversation to produce a winning culture—which is the key to your organization's long term survival."

--Tim Sanders, former Chief Solutions Officer at Yahoo! and author of *Love Is the Killer App: How To Win Business and Influence Friends*

"Coffman & Sorensen make a definitive case that real culture change can only come about through a combination of a *head and heart* approach. Unless the head is connected to a *heart* which is stimulated and pumping there can be no change in performance. Attempting to lead change without reading Coffman & Sorensen is like studying English without reading Shakespeare."

-Michael Hickey, SVP Delta Point, former President, AstraZeneca NL and VP, Sales AstraZeneca US

"Many believe that organizational culture is as complex as writing software code and as dull as watching paint dry. **Culture Eats Strategy for Lunch** proves both beliefs are false. This book is full of great ideas that will stimulate your thinking and help you improve your culture. Coffman and Sorensen are culture architects who give you a blueprint based on what the best companies have done and what you need to do to create a competitive culture."

-Mark Sanborn, President of Sanborn & Associates, Inc. and best-selling author of *Fred Factor, You Don't Need A Title To Be A Leader* and *Fred 2.0*

"This book will get the busiest of leader-readers to stop and think, nod in agreement, dog-ear pages and turn to others to converse about it. The authors are not just deeply experienced consultants and researchers but they are elegant wordsmiths as well. I loved their examples, analogies, twists-of-the-tongue, titles, recommendations and provocative questions. In an age of immense competition in the marketplace, this book holds a secret for those who don't just read but actually implement the suggestions offered, moving you from knowing to doing."

-Beverly Kaye, Ph.D., Founder, Career Systems Intl.; co-author of the bestselling books, *Love 'Em or Lose 'Em* and *Help Them Grow or Watch Them Go*

This book has ignited my passion and I'm making a bigger difference throughout my organization. It has made my job easier (and our customers like us more!) This is a definitive how-to-book for high performance culture.

-Bob Donegan, CEO, Classic Brands and former President Canada, Tupperware Brands

"**Culture Eats Strategy for Lunch** is especially relevant in the world of health care. The cultures in which people live and work have a profound impact on the quality of their physical and psychological well-being. Similarly, the culture within medical facilities can be a powerful force for healing or a source of great anxiety. I recommend **Culture Eats Strategy for Lunch** for all healthcare leaders who want to create a positive culture and engage the hearts and minds of their patients, staff and physicians."

-Richard Abrams, M.D., Founder & Director, Colorado Preventive Medicine

"Based on years of solid research, and grounded with experience and practical examples **"Culture"** sets the standard for building a high performance environment. Proving the old adage that "you can't fatten the cow by simply weighing it every day", the authors describe a path to the daily behaviors necessary to build and develop an engaged and productive organization. They help all of us know that it is not enough to simply believe but that we must participate."

-Mick Zangari, Ph.D., Sr. Managing Partner, CEG Worldwide; Director of Sales, Olsson Associates

"This book 'gets it' as it relates to what truly drives successful organizations. Culture needs to be defined, created and managed continuously from organizational leaders daily, to really set an organization apart from others strategically. My head was nodding in continuous agreement with the many thoughts and ideas articulated in the book on ways to enhance a company's success through culture."

-Mark Kime, former President and Chairman of On Deck Capital

"From anecdotes to appendices, case studies to "connecting points," Culture Eats Strategy for Lunch has it all. The book's authors ask us to examine our companies closely to determine where and how we've fallen short. And they give us the necessary tools to fine-tune individual and organizational capabilities."

-Marshall Goldsmith, author of the New York Times best sellers, MOJO and What Got You Here Won't Get You There; the Thinkers50 Leadership Award for Most-Influential Leadership Thinker in the World

"Organizations put so much focus on brand– what we want to stand for in the hearts and minds of our customers. However, if our employees do not have a common set of beliefs and values, the brand simply cannot achieve its strategic goals."

-Laurie Wooden, Chief Marketing and Development Officer, Hostelling International; formerly VP of New Business Innovation and Brand Strategy, The Ritz-Carlton Hotel Company

CULTURE
Eats
STRATEGY FOR LUNCH

THE SECRET OF EXTRAORDINARY RESULTS
Igniting the Passion Within

CURT W. COFFMAN / KATHIE SORENSON, PH.D.

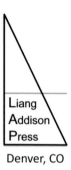

Liang
Addison
Press

Denver, CO

Printed in the United States of America
First Printing: September 2013

Library of Congress Cataloging-in-Publication Data

Coffman, Curt.
Culture Eats Strategy for Lunch: The Secret to Extraordinary Results
Igniting the Passion Within
Curt Coffman and Kathie Sorensen. p. cm.

ISBN - 13: 978-0-615-57796-8
ISBN - 10: 01615577962

1. Organizational culture
2. Leadership
3. Management
4. Employee Engagement
5. Employee Attitude Surveys

Book design by Bookdesigners, Inc.
Illustrations by Zach Walz, Jason Walton and Paula Sykora

DEDICATION

To the tradition and memory of our hero and guide, Peter
Drucker, whose quip "Culture Eats Strategy for Breakfast"
inspired us to codify how culture can be used to ignite human
passion and become a true competitive advantage.

To Tammy and to Jim, who inspire us moment by moment,
through their belief and faith, and for putting up with us.

TABLE OF CONTENTS

Section Two:

MICROCULTURE - IGNITING POSITIVE ENERGY

22 That is precisely why rabid fans always know the intricate details of their teams and follow the associated news stories so closely; they are intensely interested in everything related to the culture. Many organizations wish their associates took such a passionate interest.

23 "WE'RE LIKE A FAMILY HERE" - AND OTHER CULTURAL MISCONCEPTIONS.

24 As the family's culture interacts with the individual's unique talents, there becomes, or fails to become, a sweet spot, which unleashes and develops the inherent potential of the person.

25 THE PEOPLE YOU ATTRACT, THE PEOPLE YOU KEEP—CULTURES ARE FLUID; THEY RIPPLE WITH EACH ARRIVAL AND DEPARTURE.

25 Talent acquisition and retention are as critical to culture as fuel is to a combustion engine.

26 Who wants to belong to a group that anyone can join? Certainly not the best-in-class.

26 The entire organization experiences problems caused by poor employees and often has issues with management that fails to act.

27 WHAT DO WE REALLY NEED FROM OUR MICROCULTURE? UNIVERSAL AND INDIVIDUAL NEEDS AT WORK.

27 People must be clear about the desired outcomes of their role and see the value of their contributions.

27 If you did your job perfectly, what results would you see?

28 Some metrics are pseudo-outcomes, which provide the illusion of measurement but can lead us to unprofitable or ineffective actions relative to our real goals.

29 When people know the real outcomes of their work, they are able to determine the right thing to do without confusing the metric with the end result.

29 Excellence evolves from purpose.

30 You can't create passion, but you can destroy it with a stick or a shrug.

30 People must feel they have a productive two-way relationship with their manager and team.

31 All relationships matter to engagement, but in terms of importance, it is the manager/immediate supervisor who has the greatest influence on the person's effectiveness, tenure, and growth.

33 People need to feel utilized and develop their talents to reach new levels of success.

34 What if our personal drive to win—our capability—is subverted by a culture that overlooks the individual?

Section Three:

BRIDGECULTURE - CONNECTING PEOPLE TO PURPOSE

Section 4:
MACROCULTURE - BEING MORE INTERESTED THAN INTERESTING

But customers who resist our products, advice, council, service, and representatives can make hostages of our people and diminish our culture.

Section Five:
WHAT TO DO ABOUT IT - CREATING COMPETITIVE ADVANTAGE

APPENDIX

CULTURE

Eats

STRATEGY FOR LUNCH

Section One
STRANDED IN A SEA OF MISSED-CONNECTIONS

The scene opens:
> *One man (Tom Hanks sans the volleyball) stands on a small sandy outcrop in the ocean. His only possession—his DNA and what knowledge and skills he has picked up along the way.*

> *He has goals:*
> - *A happy family.*
> - *Meaningful work.*
> - *A chance to make a difference.*

> *But these goals continue to elude him, alone on his island. He doesn't have the tools, talent or know-how to get his needs met.*

> *We feel for Tom, a victim of his circumstances.*

The camera pans out and shows us the "rest of the story."
> *Tom's sandy beach is a desk in the middle of the second floor in a five-story office building. A sea of cubicles, quiet little keystrokes and the people who make them, surround him. Each person is isolated, separate, alone. Occasionally someone gets up to grab a cup of coffee. Tension hangs in the air; the mood is somber, the energy non-existent. The shared purpose? 5 pm, quitting time.*

Things are different on the 4th floor. Well, the cubicles and jobs are the same, but not the feeling.
> *Like a magnet, Mary's desk pulls in people, their dreams and their talents. It is a hub in the buzz of the room, intense, collaborative, and productive. Sounds of people laughing waft up from cubicles and coffee pot. The energy is palpable as people celebrate the little victories in working together and in the mission they share.*

Research suggests that a full 35 percent of people feel alienated at work, working around people but never really connected to them. But this is not about the work—it's about the *workplace*.

What's it like where you work?
Does your workplace suck the life out of you? Or are you one of the lucky ones, the 42% whose work life fills you with a sense of accomplishment, partnership and joy?

We don't change that much, but our cultures do!
Our DNA is what it is—we don't have the opportunity (at least yet) to "swap

it out" for better genes. Our talents are "hardwired"—but our environment is highly variable:

A small boy. A new school. A bad teacher = an eager boy stifled, uncertain, and lonely.

A young woman. Trusting coworkers. A great manager = a confident woman encouraged, productive and happy.

The world we find ourselves in either enhances or diminishes our life, our growth and our contribution.

All culture is personal. And so is this story.

We were blessed to have experienced great culture. As young professionals, in the beginning of our careers we were each, separately drawn to a small organization with a huge promise: to help us understand our unique talents and put them to vital and productive use. It was there that we learned the building blocks of great organizational culture first hand: Individual talent, trusting relationships, and the right expectations.

These fundamentals were celebrated in Curt's first, best-selling book, *First Break All the Rules, What the world's greatest managers do differently* (co-authored with Marcus Buckingham), and his next, *Follow this Path, How the world's greatest organizations drive growth by unleashing human potential (*co-authored with Gabriel Gonzalez-Molina*).*

We both credit the culture of that organization for nearly three decades of personal and professional growth. It accentuated our strengths and brought out the best in us. We came to know the power of belonging and the exhilaration in pursuing a shared mission. We reveled in the challenge, sense of ownership and the partnership we had with colleagues. We saw our goals become accomplishments and dreamed bigger.

In words made famous by Texas Hold 'Em Poker: we were "all in."

What we didn't fully appreciate at the time was the delicate balance within culture.

If you've ever used a carpenter's level to hang a picture, you know the importance of keeping the "bubble" centered between the lines. A fraction of movement sends the bubble careening off to the side, a tiny change with major consequences to the final product.

Great culture is a state of being; it is energy in motion.

Like all energy, great culture can't be stored and saved for later. The energy within is either productively used or squandered. When the culture "bubble" goes off center it drags down individual hopes, organizational results and global competitiveness.

Little detractors start dragging the culture off kilter; decisions are made too far from the action and rules replace communication. Politics substitute for relationships and self-interest wins out over shared mission and purpose. People are divided, as the competition focuses inward.

If you don't experience excellence, average looks pretty good.

Whatever you want for your life or your children's, it is a journey you can't take alone. Who and how you connect makes all the difference. That's why the role we each play in building and maintaining a great culture is so important.

> Culture is not a situation—it is an opportunity to be "all in."
> ✦

Our destinies are tied to our cultures.

Four generations of Americans have proven their worth in the legacy to their children: their kids have exceeded the standards set by their parents. This is our right, isn't it – to expect that our children will reap the benefit from the world we had a hand in creating?

We love to be bested by those we love.

As parents, we find an immense sense of satisfaction in our children's struggle to "best us" – to demonstrate that they are smarter, more compassionate and more capable than we.

The transition from child to adult has never been easy to watch. But now, today, it is terrifying. We are being told that we are about to become the first generation whose children will not achieve our standard of living—nor experience a plethora of opportunities for employment and growth. It shocks us and appalls us that this is happening on "our watch."

Today, an industry-staffing expert shared this statistic: 53 percent of college graduates in the US are moving home after graduation—and some 83% are unemployed or under employed. We could describe this as a national tragedy, but as parents, these statistics are almost too personal for us.

We have colleagues, friends, and neighbors (many of whom are Baby Boomers), who, at the height of their careers have lost their high-paying jobs once, and then again, to less skilled or inexperienced employees. No longer managers, leaders, or directors, they are reeling from the loss of self-definition perhaps more than from the loss of income. We are speechless to console them, for we, too, see them as victims of unforeseen and unmanageable circumstances.

And what of the Millennials (born after 1982)? They have never worked in a great or healthy economy. Not to be stalled, they are racking up advanced degrees as substitutes for real jobs. Admirable, but advanced degrees seem unlikely solutions for today's culture problems.

The economic realities today are "equal opportunity fears"— they unite us all.

We have written this book for all generations (Boomers, Gen Xers, and Millenials) that must solve the culture crisis in America. This is the only time we will refer to you by group. We choose not to separate us with labels. No matter what your age, voting preference or line-of work, you are in this with us.

In the best of cultures there exists a tension between the individual and the organization. The secret to great culture lies within this tension.

In the course of our research and soul search we came to an enlightened understanding of the real issues in developing high performance cultures. We are not simply victims—"Make a Deal" losers, destined to pick the wrong job and get the pointy-haired boss. We are moment-to-moment architects of our workplaces—our own cultures.

To get what you want from culture you must give the best of yourself to it.

A WORD ABOUT THE RESEARCH
Our research has spanned over three decades and six continents with millions of individuals, thousands of managers and working teams, across volunteer organizations, small businesses and mega-corporations. We are continually seeking to extrapolate and verify our findings across contexts and methodologies.

Our consulting with leaders, managers, sales executives and with students, colleagues and friends has put real faces to our research, resulting in a whole new reverence for the myriad of cultures to which we each belong.

For that reason, we have deliberately provided a wider range of cultural examples i.e., shared references (the media, movie stars and other national disappointments and successes). We want you to see this amazing phenomenon we so casually refer to as "culture" in all its power to affect the quality of our lives.

STRATEGY IS THE PROMISE THAT CULTURE MUST DELIVER

Nature is clear. So is business: evolve or die.

Like the dinosaurs before us, business giants are tumbling from their perch—Arthur Andersen, Circuit City, Hostess, and many more. Some are gone completely; others cling to a gray half-life that keeps them at the brink of the economic tar pit. To survive in this new economy, many companies have placed their faith in strategy, brand, and innovation. Yet time and again, even the best plans fall short of their potential and the companies end up where they began. We have discovered that in the majority of these cases what goes wrong isn't the strategy; rather, success or failure is a result of the organization's culture.

We refer to the chasm between organizational dreams and present reality as the "strategy gap." The distance across that gap is the province of culture.

Effective culture is like a six-lane suspension bridge, and poor culture is like a swinging bridge strung together with fraying rope.

The gap between our goals and our results has prompted a call to realign culture with strategy. But what does that mean? And where does the realignment occur?

Perhaps you are expecting us to say: At the top! If so, you are going to be disappointed. Realigning culture with strategy can't be done at the top because the energy to act exists deep within the organization.

The brand promise may be crafted at the strategy level, but it is the organization's culture that either delivers or breaks that promise.

We have come to understand the underlying values of a culture, its history and deeply held traditions as its religion. When strategy conflicts with the bedrock – you can expect disappointments:

> *Sintro[1] had a deep sense of tradition and a distinguished history yet was failing both financially and with its customers. The (external) board installed a new CEO—a well-qualified, talented individual with a well-defined strategy—to address the problems and bring new vision.*

---

[1] The names of organizations and individuals have been changed throughout the book to preserve the confidentiality of our sources. Although the examples reflect actual organizations, "Sintro" and the other names we have selected do not apply to any organization by that name.

The Sintro culture declined the offer to change.

The board tried again—new, improved CEO, shiny new plan.

The culture declined the offer.

Not twice, but five times in four years the Sintro culture prevailed over the newly appointed CEOs and the change plans-de-jour.

Cultures don't change on leader demand.

While leadership presides over the organization's strategy, the people themselves are the key to its energy. And people are emotional.

In the above example, the culture did change, but not in the direction intended by leadership. Over the five-year saga, the culture became more resistant to leadership's efforts. The people became increasingly suspicious of any change initiated from the top or outside and steadily more confident in their own ability to wait out the next leader.

Culture at the broader organizational level, what we call *MacroCulture*, appears to take on the shape of its leadership. But upon closer examination, culture actually *reflects* the smaller groups within, what we term *MicroCulture*. This is the first thing that you should know about creating high-performance cultures—you can't drive them from the top.

No people - no culture.

The people create the culture's energy—working together in teams, work units, departments, and small groups; they are the life force of the organization.

An organization doesn't have a single culture, but about as many MicroCultures as there are people.

Healthy, vital MicroCultures are the heartbeat of the organization, the energy available to fuel goals and objectives. People connect to the larger organization and its mission through the MicroCultures they're involved with, the most significant being the local culture associated with the work unit. However, any formal or informal group has its own MicroCulture. It could be the sales department, or it could be the group on the third floor who take lunch together on Tuesdays.

To manage culture, leaders often take a scalpel to it.

Structural change is a vehicle of leader convenience. Leaders naturally find it easier to dismantle things they can't manage and substitute new (hopefully more effective) arrangements. Enter Mother Organization wielding her spreadsheet-engineered elements like downsizings, plant closings, layoffs, and reorganizations, which bring the promise of future efficiency and focus.

A high-tech organization we'll call TWTroon embraced a new strategy that depended on their ability to move from product to solution sales. They studied their best sales professionals and determined that they were highly solution focused.

TWT decided to require every incumbent salesperson to re-apply for their job. Leadership expected this would result in a sales force that epitomized best practices.

For eighteen months, their best salespeople continued to work, selling to and servicing their customers. One of their top performers, Sam, said, "Things are so screwed up at corporate, the only way to get anything done around here is to fly under the radar."

In spite of counsel to the contrary, the organization did little to attend to its top producers during this time of change; they forced all employees, including Sam, through the new selection process like sheep to the dip. Their most talented and effective salespeople (never happy to be sheep) left them for new opportunities with competitors.

Some of the organization's best customers followed the salespeople who had earned their loyalty.

What started as a strategy to enhance sales effectiveness backfired in a huge way.

Culture doesn't tolerate shortcuts.

Blame the organizational chart. As the skeletal system of the organization, it is responsible for much of our confusion and consternation over culture.

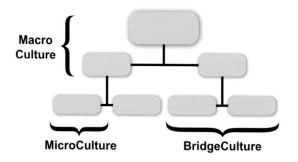

On the organizational chart, our reporting relationships are meticulously described with solid and dotted lines. They are the rational explanation for how the organization works.

But these charts rarely describe our real connections with one another— our emotional connections. When leaders tamper blindly with people's roles, there can be a hefty price to pay.

In the aforementioned case, trust was lost between the sales force and leadership; anxiety drained energy from not just the sales force, but from the groups supporting them. The organization lost time, talent, and market share, leaving them in the precarious position of rebuilding what they had lost before they had even begun to realize any gain from the new structure.

The connection between our MicroCultures and the larger purpose of the organization is the BridgeCulture.

It is not a separate single culture, but again reflects the numerous ways in which we link teams, groups, and departments into effective and productive work flows.

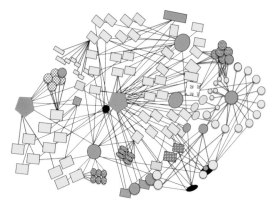

The organizational hierarchy, roles, and procedures are all a part of the BridgeCulture, but it is the human interaction within these structures— our emotional connections—that determines its effectiveness. Whenever people experience organizational processes, policies, or procedures, the outcome is either inspiring or defeating.

Imagine an announcement, which unilaterally eliminated working from home in an organization known for its virtual workforce! Messages from the CEO sometimes bypass the bridge entirely – and not always to best advantage.

The quality of interdepartmental synergy, or the lack thereof, is a test of BridgeCulture effectiveness. Think of BridgeCultures as the connective tissue between muscle groups. When the synapses are firing in sync, problems become opportunities. But when there is a lack of communication, partnership, or relationships, the energy is wasted, creating schisms instead of bridges.

The BridgeCulture connects people to purpose, either igniting their passion or squandering their energy in the process.

BridgeCulture fractures occur in the absence of relationship, sense of purpose, and shared outcomes. This divides the culture into groups of *them and us*. Each side's perception of the *other group* as unresponsive, unworldly, or self-serving allows them to discount the other group's perspective and perpetuates the us-versus-them mentality.

When this happens, fences go up between groups, cooperation ceases, and performance is derailed. Many organizations struggle to deal with the ramifications.

The love/hate relationship of sales and marketing is a classic example. Marketing is about sending the message up the flagpole; sales are about the direct relationship with the customer. Consider the following example from a Northeastern pharmaceutical organization:

> *In the history of the organization, senior leadership had always come from the sales channel.*

> *When the new senior leader, Bob, arrived via the marketing side of the business, the company strategy, financial investment and focus shifted. The financial and human resources were increasingly devoted to advertising and brand positioning.*

> *As sales territories were adjusted and the sales force downsized, the sales organization felt minimized, referring to the new approach as the "tail wagging the dog."*

Success depends on the quality of the relationship between the different groups, not simply their individual actions. Both sides desire the same ultimate outcome. The best results are produced when the overall true purpose is clarified and shared.

> *Our heart and lungs have singular functions and each must fulfill its unique obligations. Yet ultimately our very survival is dependent upon their ability to work together.*

Managers are the translators, the connectors, and the catalysts of MicroCultures and BridgeCultures.

One of the most fascinating aspects of culture research is that the ranges *within* organizations almost always exceed the range *between* them.
In a single physical environment, with the same products, services and policies, and essentially the same jobs and work, we invariably see a huge variation in the quality of micro and bridge cultures. Why? Searching for the common denominator we find the manager. The manager's impact is so great that people tend to leave managers, not organizations.

The Great Manager is a cultural force for good. One of the most successful hockey coaches of all time was asked about his greatest satisfaction. One might have expected him to mention the Stanley Cup, but his comments instead made clear WHY he was so successful:

> *"Getting out on the ice with young players."*

He had the heart of a true developer, one whose focus is on the individual. A great manager interprets the individual's talent in a way that maximizes that person's strength, contribution and growth. Rules and policies are translated in a way that makes them work for the people and the customer. The great manager is a bridge builder.

The most effective BridgeCultures are built around line-of-sight with the customer, which is the single commonality able to connect the goals of the entire workforce.

Every day and every hour, each individual should see how their job impacts two things: the acquisition of new customers and the retention of current customers. If they can't, they are in a "non-job." This is line-of-sight!

Often one of the greatest cultural challenges within an organization is to create bridges solid enough to support innovation and top-notch customer service. An interesting example comes to us from one of the most trusted names in hospitality, electing to embark on a new strategy in the vacation time-share market. This pillar of hospitality with more than fifty years of brand experience left three families stranded at Christmastime when their new policy collided with their passion for service.

> *Three generations of Caldwells booked and paid for a holiday reunion in May. When the time arrived to use it, the first family to arrive was turned away. The family member who booked the units was delayed due to flight problems and although the accommodations were 1) fully paid for, 2) designated to family members and 3) available, a "booking technicality" made checking in impossible they were told.*

The technicality? The family's vacation was booked through an authorized third-party, not with the actual company.

Acknowledging the obvious conflict between the policy and the right thing to do, the clerk pleaded for their understanding, saying, "I know you are right, and I really want to help you! But if I let you check in, I could lose my job."

Unfortunately for the Caldwells, left accommodation-less in the parking lot, the organization's policy took precedence over their long-standing commitment to customer service.

In companies' efforts to preserve their standards, they create policies, procedures, and scripting. These strategies often execute at the local level and prevent intelligent, service-oriented people from doing what they do best: making it right for their guests.

We can all guess what happened to the customer's loyalty in this example.

But what happened to the desk clerk?

Caught in the crosshairs between the business process and the brand promise, her faith in each was shaken. At a moment when her line-of-sight with the customers should have freed her to act in their best interest, she was left powerless to take action.

What companies gain in speed (making rules and policies), they often lose in energy, focus, and results.

For over thirty years, our research with highly productive cultures and their less successful counterparts has helped us to see culture as energy, both productive and nonproductive. Wholesale attempts to legislate new strategies into existence always incur trade-offs. The process wreaks havoc on the cultural landscape, and the energy becomes acidic, leaking at the seams and tainting everything in its wake.

> When people become disillusioned at work, statistics suggest they:
> - Quit
> - Stay and work to make things different; or
> - Become ROAD warriors (Retired on Active Duty)

Leadership strategies, structure, and rules take a pretty big bite out of culture!

At this moment in history, many organizational cultures are fractured, overrun with anxiety and hamstrung with rules that prevent good people from doing the right thing. Copious amounts of human energy and capital have been spent in an effort to get ahead of human frustration and fear.

Some nonproductive cultures are starving for a vision or central focus; others are wasting the energy of their people by regularly changing and manipulating the direction of their focus. Most contemporary companies are suffering from an assault on their basic expectations. Like the desk clerk, we have collectively learned not to trust and have developed a kind of *shared helplessness*.

Organizations, in spite of their intentions to the contrary, strip the passion right out of the people...and the people are the culture.

Strategies are born through rational processes. They often look better in theory than they do in real life. Why? Because the people are the culture, and people are messy!

Culture is what results from the collision of the rational with the emotional.

These collisions are moment-by-moment connections—what we call *touchpoints*—in the life of the organization. Culture is not a single entity, nor a dichotomy of formal/informal cultures, but a myriad of Micro- and BridgeCultures that reflect the individuals, groups, departments, and divisions of our organizations. These MicroCultures, as experienced by the people within, flex continuously like a pulse of energy.

Culture is not the enemy of strategy and performance, but an equal player in the game, not to be underestimated or overlooked.

For each organization, there exists a crucial connection point where the business promise hinges on the culture. Our competition can copy our products, methods, and service, they can hire our stars, duplicate our marketing, use our vendors, and lure our customers with amazing offers, but they can't clone the culture that created these advantages.

It is the emotional nature of culture that renders it capable of becoming your worst nightmare or your most sustainable competitive advantage.

This book is about the precarious balance between two forces—rational and emotional—that intertwine to create culture at every level of the organization. Our touchpoints, strategies, and tactics can either take a *bite* out of our culture or ignite the passion within it. As leaders, managers, and employees, we must choose to be active owners of the cultures to which we belong to draw out the best of the cultures' qualities and align them to our business imperatives.

We must learn how to:
- *Ignite the passion in ourselves and our people.*
- *Connect our people to each other, our mission, and purpose.*
- *Revitalize our cultures as a competitive advantage for our organizations, ourselves, and our families.*

Our individual and collective futures depend on this challenge, making the cultures in which we work and live a personal issue for all of us. To experience passion at work, to see our businesses flourish, we must begin with our individual connection: *MicroCulture, where you just can't wait to come to work!*

✢ ✢ ✢

MICROCULTURE: IGNITING POSITIVE ENERGY

Cheers!

*Making your way in the world today takes everything you've got.
Taking a break from all your worries sure would help a lot.
Wouldn't you like to get away?*

*Sometimes you want to go…where everybody knows your name,
and they're always glad you came.*

We always smile when we hear the theme song for the TV program *Cheers*. No specific word or sentence moves us; it is the general essence of the message. It touches the need we all share to feel welcome—to belong. Something as small as just being remembered, having someone know your name, creates a sense of worth. In return, we feel compelled to pass it on.

We all want to have that place where we feel unique, supported, and not judged. These places allow us to think acceptingly of ourselves; we value the time we spend there, we get a glimpse of another person's uniqueness and even stand in awe of them. It's not about what the person does or has accomplished, but about who that person is and of what he or she is capable of.

These characters—Norm, Cliff, Frasier and his wife Lilith, Sam, Diane, Carla, and Woody—didn't just step into a bar; they entered, created, and nurtured a culture.

Attraction is a powerful emotion critical to healthy culture; it drives us forward, toward something we want to be a part of. Under the spell of attraction, we are drawn to take risks, some of which work out and some of which do not, but the experience itself enriches our lives forever.

We all crave experiences that will truly change us, feed our hunger for seeing things differently, and broaden our perspective. We need challenges to release our own conventional point of view and provide an opportunity for a paradigm shift. Then, when a new perspective finally hits and fills a gap we hadn't previously recognized, the experience is exhilarating and we become stronger, more confident people.

We all need a place where we can drop our defenses and be vulnerable; these are the places where our most significant relationships are born. When people feel a strong sense of belonging, they say, "I love it here" or "I can't wait to come back."

Culture is the common core that creates belonging, influences our actions, and shapes who we become.

The koi, a multicolored Japanese fish, is one such example. Its size is solely determined by the size of the pond in which it lives. The ecosystem actually defines what this beautiful creature will become.

When we apply this natural law to ourselves, it begs these questions: What cultures have we placed ourselves in, and how have these cultures influenced who we are today? A professor we know once asked his class:

"Does anyone here know how to make a mouse?" Many were baffled, and one person quipped that "only God could make a mouse." But the professor disagreed. He went on to say that it is actually quite simple. "Go to your basement, throw an old flannel shirt on the floor, throw some flour and a few chunks of cheese down, and soon a mouse will appear."

While many organizations aim to create a culture that produces incredible outcomes, they forget that it is the shirt, flour, and cheese that attract the mouse.

The best cultures can't be forced—they can only be made to attract.

Why is it that some spiritual communities seemingly expand overnight? Is it the inspirational message of the leader, or is it the rewarding feeling of being trusted and contributing to something larger than oneself? Take a look at Alcoholics Anonymous, one of the fastest growing organizations in recent history.[2] Members of Alcoholics Anonymous report an overwhelming sense of peace and well-being when they attend meetings, because everyone there has a shared problem and purpose—no pretense or defense, just a shared desire to help one another. As one AA member told us "we're all here because we aren't all there."

Organizations today are facing a very difficult challenge:

How do we create a culture that people really want to be a part of, feel an emotional connection to, and in which they feel compelled to create exceptional outcomes?

---

[2] AA (Alcoholic Anonymous) is an excellent example of a deliberate and successful culture. Founded in 1935 with two members, today more than two million call themselves members. There are more than 100,000 AA groups that meet regularly throughout the world.

THE POWER OF CULTURE COMES FROM THE PEOPLE WITHIN.

You hop in the car, take the same route to work, park in the same space, enter the same door, proceed to the coffee pot and catch the next elevator. You have now arrived at work; you sip your beverage and check your position on the Culture Map.

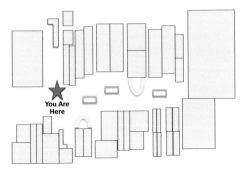

You Are Here

*The **You Are Here** icon is flashing at the intersection of **My Boss Doesn't Have a Clue** and **He Never Will**, in the vicinity of **Wasting My Talents**.*

Ouch—bad neighborhood for self-concept! You steer in a different direction.

*You thumb in a new destination: **Directions to My Dream**.*

System Error 404z: You can't get there from here.

Well, that bites, you think to yourself.

*You take a deep breath, scale back your expectations for the day, and thumb in a new destination: **My Customers Get What They Need**.*

System Error 404z2: You can't get there from here.

*A little desperate now, you go for what should be an easy destination: **Have a Fairly OK Day**.*

System Error 404z3: You'll never get there from here.

Decades of organizational data suggest that approximately one out of every three employees currently works at the corner of Helpless and Victim.[1] If the above navigational system for the culture maze in which we live and work actually existed, almost one-third of all employees would be in a panic.

What does it mean to be engaged at work? It means the person sees the value of what they do every day and that they are working on teams with people they like and trust.

The opposite is true for others: their work is not a "fit" to their talents and they often feel unproductive, misunderstood and alienated from their manager and co-workers. This is not just bad for the person, but bad for their life outside of work.

The personal toll for bad culture is more than people can afford to pay.

It's estimated that employees bring their work problems home at six times the rate they bring their home problems to work. Functioning in this type of energy-sucking vortex makes people question their worth and sours life for themselves and their families.

The negative impact on the person and their family is just one of the penalties of poor culture; the organizational and economic costs are astronomical as well.

Corporations spend an estimated 11 billion dollars on turnover, much of which can be attributed to bad management/poor culture.[2] While the methodology among researchers varies, there is little disagreement that employee turnover is a multibillion dollar problem. The costs include the obvious practical expenses like advertising, recruiting, interviewing, hiring, and onboarding of new talent, and the opportunity loss relative to customers and performance.

The leading cause of turnover? Poor people management in the MicroCulture, says the data from thousands of exit interviews and research. Our research suggests 30 percent of people leave their organizations because of a disconnection in the micro culture.[3]

Discussions about employee engagement have been on the radar since the late 1990's, when the relationship of engagement to performance was established. We were particularly interested in uncovering the elements of MicroCulture that lead to higher performance.

The figure below summarizes our research with nine elements that systematically differentiate microcultures that have better talent retention, fewer lost work days, better margin growth, better sales growth, higher customer engagement and retention and better individual growth.

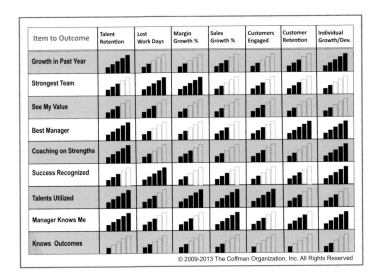

Item to Outcome	Talent Retention	Lost Work Days	Margin Growth %	Sales Growth %	Customers Engaged	Customer Retention	Individual Growth/Dev.
Growth in Past Year							
Strongest Team							
See My Value							
Best Manager							
Coaching on Strengths							
Success Recognized							
Talents Utilized							
Manager Knows Me							
Knows Outcomes							

Every item shown above is associated with high performance MicroCultures. Since 2006, over a million people have been interviewed about the factors that create engagement and the results reveal three distinct groups:

The Actively Engaged: *Individuals who consistently perform at significantly higher levels across outcome measures. They enthusiastically drive productive relationships with customers and associates. Continuous improvement and innovation are a personal quest.*

Passengers: *Individuals in a holding pattern who tend to meet the minimum requirements of the job. Indifferent, slower adapters who wait for others to act, we think of them as "passengers" rather than activators in the work environment.*

The Actively Dis-engaged: *They are unhappy and actively share it. The focus of their relationships is built on the negative; they co-sign other people's discontent with no exploration of solutions.*

Our latest research reflects these percentages:
2013: 42% Actively Engaged 23% Passengers, and 35% Actively Dis-engaged.

Does that mean that everyday we are working at 42% of potential?

In review of this data with a professor at one of the top business schools, he put things in perspective:

> *This data means that only four out of every ten-branch banks would be open for business, if only Actively Engaged people came to work.*

Organizations tend to measure human energy in terms of FTEs (Full Time Equivalents), but people and their effectiveness at work are much more variable than that term would imply.

What are the implications of poor microcultures on the energy available to the organization to drive business results? Some experts, Blanchard[4], for example, estimate that employees work at about 70 percent of capacity. Our research average is actually a bit lower (65 percent).

But the real story here is reflected in the variation of energy between the *actively engaged* and the *actively dis-engaged*:

> *Research indicates that actively engaged people are functioning at high levels of purposeful energy, reporting that they are able to use 82 percent of their talents and abilities at work.*

> *In contrast, the actively dis-engaged are functioning at only 27 percent of their capacity.*

These statistics may temp us to describe the actively dis-engaged as "inactively dis-engaged," but the reality is that energy is being expended, just not productively.

Consider the ramifications of this variation from a project management perspective, where our strategies reflect some basic assumptions aka FTEs:

> *A team of 100 people working 40 hours a week is 4000 staff hours.*

> *If on average only 42 are "engaged" at work, their useful, productive staff time drops accordingly (perhaps by as much as 41%).*

FTEs	100 People	40 Hrs/Wk	Capacity	= 4000 staff hours
Actively Engaged	42	40	@ .82	1378
Passengers	23	40	@ .65	598
Actively Dis-engaged	35	40	@ .27	378
Productive energy				2354 staff hours

When teams are comprised of the Actively Engaged, Passengers and
Actively Dis-engaged, the end results suffer.

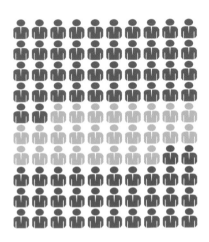

*Companies typically experience the energy
loss associated with poor MicroCulture
in the gap between their plans and their
results.*

*IT industry experts tell us only 4 of every 10
planned upgrades are delivered in the first
release to the customer.*

*Is this so surprising when you consider that
4/10 people are truly actively engaged at
work?*

Research comparing planned budgets, benefits and timelines against actual
results for 1,471 IT projects, reported in the Harvard Business Review,
revealed an average cost overrun of 27 percent. Even more significantly,
one in six projects incurred (on average) a whopping cost overrun of
200 percent! One project, budgeted at $5 million ended up costing the
company nearly $200 million and never delivered the projected benefits.[5]

Could your organization absorb an overrun of 200 percent?

Once the overruns occur, the damage is done. What would it be worth to
be able to map productive energy real time?   Priceless.

People bring their talent, vitality, and inspiration to work every day, but
these gifts are either used or wasted, depending on the culture:

• *Energy directed to the organization's goals is positive, purposeful,
and productive for the organization and the individual.*

- *Energy spent by distractions, worry, and frustration can't be recovered—by the organization or the individual.*

The best way for an organization to ignite the purposeful energy of its people is through each person's sense of belonging and value. This is directly dependent on the MicroCulture because that's where the energy resides. That energy begins with each individual and his or her connection to the team and manager.

✦ ✦ ✦

EVERY PERSON IS MULTICULTURAL IT'S BELONGING THAT MATTERS.

At the end of the day, cultures reflect the people within them and their connection with one another. These cultures are overlapping circles of relationships. We are fathers, sons, brothers, and at the same time we are Presbyterian, American, and Hispanic.

Every person is multicultural, and beneath the most visible popular cultures, there are also countless subcultures, which may be surprising or unique. We offer: Star Trekkies – original series, male O.R. nurses, and teensy-weensy NBA players, some with great names like Muggsy Bogues.[6]

Each culture we participate in holds us to a set of beliefs or values. When our various cultures are in sync with one another, our world is copacetic because the rules we live by align; our relationships are simpatico and we are able to exist in the intermingling circles without angst. When our cultures align with our values, we experience satisfaction and confidence.

Unlike gravity, a culture's pull on us is dependent on our commitment to it; the more important it is for us to belong, the stronger the pull.

If we avow membership, the culture's influence is the strongest and we are deeply affected by its evolution (or deterioration, based on our view).

Take the Oakland Raider's *Raider Nation*, for example. One would be hard-pressed to find a more rabid set of fans, complete with their swords, chains, and pirate patches. But the *Raider Nation* is much more than the Fan Code of Conduct on the Raiders website:[7]

> ### Fan Code of Conduct:
> *Help us create the most fan-friendly environment in the NFL.*
> *We want all fans to enjoy the action and excitement of Oakland Raiders football...*

The above code is written in such a bland tone that it could speak to any sports team, making us wonder if the lawyers were involved. It really doesn't do justice to this unique set of fans.

Whether the fans are at the stadium, in the parking lot, or in the family room, they experience the de facto Raider culture. It's a culture that persists regardless of the team's win/loss record because it's the *belonging* that counts most, not the outcome. Interestingly, Raiders fans are such a powerful culture that a whole new subculture emerged in response: the Official Raider Haters Universe.[8]

The drive to belong binds the person to the culture and makes that culture, and everything within it, really matter.

That is precisely why rabid fans always know the intricate details of their teams and follow the associated news stories so closely; they are intensely interested in everything related to the culture. Many organizations wish their associates took such a passionate interest.

In terms of organizational culture, we can only imagine the joy in the boardroom if our customers demonstrated this level of affinity toward our culture regardless of our product's performance. Instead, many organizations struggle to make even their *paid associates* care about the culture.

There could be many objections to the Oakland Raiders example, among them that the Oakland Raiders fans are volunteers, while our associates are employed. But paid or unpaid, a strong culture has the capability of attracting its members. You can't buy a sense of belonging.

The key is *belonging,* and that is always an individual choice.

✛ ✛ ✛

"WE'RE LIKE A FAMILY HERE" AND OTHER CULTURAL MISCONCEPTIONS.

Over the course of thousands of conversations about culture, perhaps the most prevalent description we hear is "family." Why? Well-intentioned people are likely attempting to communicate what they see as the *connectedness* of their organization, its appreciation for its members and their longevity, and—at least to some degree—relationships of warmth, trust, and support.

> A hospital's slogan on a billboard read:
> **TREATING YOU LIKE FAMILY.**
> Noting the billboard a woman remarked:
> "If they treat me like my family treats me, I'll NEVER go there!"
>
> ✦

In spite of the frequency, *family* isn't an optimal adjective for organizational culture. We don't really argue with the sentiment, but the focus of family is predominantly internal (the health, safety, and growth of its members), while the focus of organizations must be predominantly external, rooted in the acquisition and retention of its customers.

Organizations exist for a compelling reason: to service the customer. It's an external focus. Members are in good standing when they contribute toward that outcome, and they are in poor standing when they fail to contribute.

That said, we can still learn a bit from the prevalence of the term *family* as a descriptor. Family means something unique to each of us. More importantly, we can borrow from family research to make some valid and telling assertions about the essence of culture and, more specifically, the inherently individual nature of culture.

Research with siblings growing up in happy, well-adjusted homes reveals the true nature of the individual's interaction with the culture: it is never the same for any of us.

Growing up around the dinner table, we are tempted to believe we experienced the same family environment, complete with mores, values, and practices. It is only after the fact, as adults (sometimes after intense therapy) that we realize our notions of the *family* vary by the perceiver.

> *Mom, Dad, Howie, Marta, and Phil's dinner hour was always highly charged. Political observations flew back and forth over the dinner table, filling the air with heated debate from passionate advocates. It was a time when everything and nothing could be challenged. The three siblings responded exactly as they would continue to respond throughout their lives: Howie skillfully avoiding the volleys, gaining*

*practice in the art of sidestep; Marta thriving in denial, defender of
peace and harmony in the house; and Phil digging in his heels, his
position always a complete 180 degrees from Dad.*

It isn't until much later—as adults, when the dust clears—that we recognize
that these common events have produced completely different family
histories depending on which sibling you ask, Howie, Marta, or Phil.

*Our family, which begins in each of our child-minds as such a
foundational rock in our belief system, is not, in fact, a rock, but a
collection of perceptions owned by each family member, and even the
innocent bystanders—neighbors, teachers, or cousins.*

**As the family's culture interacts with the individual's unique talents,
there becomes, or fails to become, a sweet spot, which unleashes
and develops the inherent potential of the person.**

The dynamics of being first-born or the infamous middle child are subject
to considerable debate, but they are clear signs that the culture of the
family has a substantive impact on the development of the individual's
relationships, achievement orientation, and creativity (among other drives
and characteristics).

Research with dysfunctional families has brought additional insight,
particularly studies regarding the destructive impact of a controlling
and abusive partner on the self-confidence of the long-suffering spouse.
Individual talent and capability can endure and even flourish in the face of
such family-culture obstacles. For example, in his autobiography, *My Life*,
Bill Clinton described confronting his stepfather's abuse with a golf club:

*Mother was on the floor and Daddy was standing over her, beating on
her. I told him to stop and said that if he didn't I was going to beat the
hell out of him with the golf club. He just caved, sitting down in a chair
next to the bed and hanging his head.*[9]

Clinton's mother, Virginia Kelley, recounted the same scene in her own
autobiography, *Leading with My Heart: My Life,* and while parallel to Bill's, the
emotional residue associated with the recollection is distinctive. Our perceptions
are always unique and so are the meanings we associate with them.

Some very talented and successful people have overcome early familial
hardships: Joe Torre's father was abusive, Barbara Streisand suffered the
loss of her father at a young age, and Oprah Winfrey spent her early years
in poverty. These special individuals faced ugliness and rose above it to

achieve amazing accomplishments. Unfortunately, many people who experience difficulties in their early childhood never fully prevail.

What does this say to our purposes? The individual's relationship to the MicroCulture—the local work unit— is critical to his or her connection to the organization. Organizations can attempt to compensate for the deficits of poor MicroCultures, but these efforts may not generate sufficient return on that investment. If a MicroCulture fails its members, there will be a significant impact on their effectiveness at work.

✦ ✦ ✦

THE PEOPLE YOU ATTRACT, THE PEOPLE YOU KEEP
CULTURES ARE FLUID; THEY RIPPLE WITH EACH ARRIVAL AND DEPARTURE.

Because cultures reflect the people within, they most vividly reflect the people who stay. High-performance organizations attract and retain people who make and keep their culture green (effective) and growing. Talented people who engage with the mission, continually developing and producing, are the lifeblood of the organization. These core members give the organization the ability to evolve and adapt to meet the needs of the marketplace.

Talent acquisition and retention are as critical to culture as fuel is to a combustion engine.

The quality and *fit* of an individual make the difference between success and failure.

> *A case in point is Zappos. This highly successful organization is known for its ability to recruit and on-board talented people who reflect their incredible service culture. While attracting talent is key, it is Zappos' commitment to insuring the right fit between the person and the demands of the role that leads to sustainability.*

> *There's such a high premium on the company's service values that they initially offered new hires $100 to quit the company if the person didn't feel the organization was right for them.*

> *Periodically, this sum was raised due to concerns that enough people weren't taking the offer; it now stands at $4,000. Zappos' leadership recognizes how important the people are to the culture that has made them so successful.*

In contrast, what happens to organizations that are not selective of their members? The ability of the organization to serve its purpose can be strained by the disparity between the values of the people and the purpose of the organization.

Who wants to belong to a group that anyone can join? Certainly not the best-in-class.

Prestigious universities and colleges provide the most pervasive example of the importance of selectivity. These premier institutions sort through thousands of applicants to identify and admit a select few. Arguably, at the top of nearly everyone's list of the best colleges and universities are the following schools:

For the freshman class in the fall of 2013:

- *Harvard University selected 6% of approximately 35,000 applications*
- *Princeton University selected 9% of 27,000 applications*
- *Yale University selected 8% of 29,000 applications*
- *Columbia University selected 7% of 35,000 applications*[10]

As these schools well appreciate, the freshman class of 2013 sets the limiting parameters on the graduates of 2017 and their alumni support in 2040. Their selection decisions will change the culture and future of the school as surely as their faculty, programs, and practices.

In the case of academic institutions, this is patently obvious, but many business organizations continue to focus more on the structural elements of their cultures than on the individual talent within. Perhaps that's because changes in structure and operations can be executed more unilaterally and evaluated more practically. It is much more difficult to assess the movement of our cultures.

Your organization's culture reflects not just the people who join, but also the people who stay. The implications of layoffs done indiscriminately are damaging to the culture, but dealing with poor performers can become an opportunity to improve confidence in leadership. As one leader described it:

"During the last layoff at Heathman & Ross, only poor performers were impacted, and there was no huge negative impact. In fact, our engagement scores went up."

The entire organization experiences problems caused by poor employees and often has issues with management that fails to act.

In this case, employees complained that supervisors had been slow to take action against low performers. After the reduction in force, management acknowledged their vision to bring the company back to better performance and then began to report progress monthly. When they delivered on the plan—which they did—this built trust.

Selection is only the beginning. For a culture to have meaning, it's essential for people to connect within it, and that means relationships. Human beings have a universal need to belong; relationship is the glue that bonds individuals to the group, and ultimately to the organization.

+   +   +

WHAT DO WE REALLY NEED FROM OUR MICROCULTURE? UNIVERSAL AND INDIVIDUAL NEEDS AT WORK.

Decades of research have yielded a very clear picture of the importance of engagement as a key measure in understanding local culture. We know that the definitive test of engagement is from the individual's perspective: we must understand how the person experiences his or her environment.

Here are some universal conditions that consistently emerge when we test engagement in the workplace. People are engaged when they:

1) Are clear about the desired outcomes of their role and see the value of their contributions.
2) Feel they have a productive two-way relationship with their manager and their team.
3) Have the opportunity to use their natural abilities and are growing to new levels of success.

How do each of these universal conditions affect the individual's energy within the MicroCulture?

People must be clear about the desired outcomes of their role and see the value of their contributions.

Every role has a set of outcomes that the position was designed to attain— the reason the position exists. When our focus waivers from the outcomes, so do our results.

If you did your job perfectly, what results would you see?

Companies often attempt to impose specific measures to provide an objective way to review their progress. Here's one hospital's experience in confusing these measures with *real outcomes*:

> *The emergency department of Mercy General defined excellence in terms of metrics, one of which was for patients to be "in and out" in two hours. The dedicated staff focused on this metric and took pride in their responsiveness.*

As is often the case, some of the challenges to their performance measures were beyond their control: the CAT scan, for example. When a patient's CAT scan didn't come back quickly enough, it detracted from the staff's score, so they would admit the patient to the hospital to preserve their metric.

When the scan finally came back and the results were negative, the patient would be released from the hospital. Unfortunately, Mercy General would not be paid because they had prematurely admitted the patient.

Moving the patient to a bed was the literal interpretation of providing excellent service in the emergency department, but it resulted in negative financial and customer outcomes.

Organizations often impose metrics like the ones above without taking the time to clarify the real outcomes with their people.

The metric *two hours* is an indicator for timely patient service in the emergency room, where the real outcomes desired are impeccable patient care in a timely and financially sustainable way, for the patient, the physician and the hospital.

Some metrics are pseudo-outcomes, which provide the illusion of measurement but can lead us to unprofitable or ineffective actions relative to our real goals.

Staff is often caught in an uncomfortable position when trying to improve their efficiency and effectiveness. The metric in the above case caused stress for staff when the CAT scans did not come back in time. This stress caused them to seek remedies that, however well intentioned, actually undermined the overall goal, and the hospital suffered financial consequences. When leadership and staff clarified the real outcomes, the problem quickly resolved itself.

People are commonly asked to follow a set of steps or series of

PRESSURE POINTS

Torn between the metrics and the patient is a frequent issue for health care professionals.

The best tell us that the patient always wins out, but the stress takes a toll on the individual. The balancing act between our performance statistics and our real outcomes drains energy from our most committed people.

+

procedures in lieu of employing their ideas, instincts, and intelligence. Our research shows—time and again—that when these steps become the primary focus, the outcome suffers and so do the people.

"Tell me what to do" is commonly heard from individuals who work within a culture like this. Energy is being expended, but compliance becomes protocol. This is an extremely dangerous position for any individual, team, or organization, as it reduces the potential for creativity, innovation, and growth. Tell-me-what-to-do cultures spend a lot of energy trying to appear active, but they're not productive because they are not connected with the real purpose or value of the work.

When people know the real outcomes of their work, they are able to determine the right thing to do without confusing the metric with the end result.

At the local level, energy and motivation come from a clear understanding of how the daily details and activities drive something bigger. Tasks are necessary, but they never define the real reason for the job.

As in all things, the emotions count more than the logic. This emotional energy comes from the individual's attachment to the organization's purpose—its *religion*. It is not about the brand or titles or positions, but about the real reason that organization exists: service to their customers. The organization's purpose provides a North Star for its members—a guidance that lifts them above the short-term frustrations and setbacks. The line-of-sight to that North Star must be clear to each individual involved, for it is the individual's sense of purpose that brings true excellence.

The more clear a person's line-of-sight is to the customer, the more efficiently that person can sort out his or her priorities and focus on the most critical activities, not just the seemingly urgent ones. Through this process, the associate's confidence increases.

Excellence evolves from purpose.

When purpose and value are not clear, people feel the stress of expectations without the satisfaction of achievement. In organizations where people can't see their connection to the big picture, it is more difficult to focus on the minute things that may have the greatest impact on the customer. Activities may be completed, but will lack a strong connection to organic growth. That being the case, these activities can wear the passion right out of people.

When people produce something with their passion, it is connected with who they really are. When they share that work with us, our response speaks volumes.

Imagine Bill, a young writer submitting work to his first editor, his eighth grade English teacher. The teacher, by either slamming the punctuation or never acknowledging Bill's creativity, could be damning a future poet laureate.

You can't create passion, but you can destroy it with a stick or a shrug.

Leaders should resist the temptation to correct things that are meaningless to the real outcomes. By continually correcting, we can end up damaging the one thing we are most committed to seeing: individual passion at work.

People must feel they have a productive two-way relationship with their manager and team.

The power of *feeling understood* encourages a level of trust that travels both ways; courageous conversations can only take place between two parties who respect and trust one another. This leads to openness and a willingness to face situations and resolve them together.

One of our greatest tendencies as human beings is to assign meaning to things. We are actually so good at it that we attach a connotation to things that happen by chance. We are left off an e-mail trail (reply all, reply all, *reply to some*), and suddenly we feel deliberately (with malice intended) shut down.

At times like these, in the absence of facts, the motives you assign to people are a reflection of your relationship with that person. When someone tells you another person has been talking about you, what do you think?

If it's a friend we trust, we know she must be saying something good.

If it is someone who doesn't know us very well at all, the mind can assign all kinds of meaning to it. So we immediately ask, "What did she say?"

When crises occur, what better support is there than a person who really knows you, cares about you, and has your back? The predisposition to trust first is an enormous asset for an organization, and it only occurs in the local culture, forged by the connections between the people.

In such situations, feedback (however unflattering) can be more readily accepted because it is seen as intended to be helpful. How many times every day do we see people react defensively to feedback that could truly help them? This results from faltering trust between the two parties.

While friends willingly anticipate and easily overlook slights, in poor relationships the perception of faults can jeopardize *everything*. Rather than being a nonissue, situations can become morale-sucking quagmires of negative energy. Relationships can change perceptions in profound ways, and perceptions are nine-tenths of reality.

> **PLOTTING TO DO GOOD**
>
> In our organization, if we don't really know, we have agreed to trust that our partners are always "plotting to do us good."
>
> We may not be there to see it or hear it, but we know it is happening moment by moment as we go about our work everyday.
>
> -Alex, VP of Operations

Recently, a medical device organization increased its overall engagement scores from the fifty-ninth to the seventy-ninth percentile in nine months, an amazing feat and a testimony to the health of the organization's culture. One department was an outlier at the thirty-first percentile. The issue? A poor relationship between two long-term employees affected leadership confidence, overall satisfaction, and engagement.

Without exception, engagement research points to the importance of relationships at work.[11]

All relationships matter to engagement, but in terms of importance, it is the manager/immediate supervisor who has the greatest influence on the person's effectiveness, tenure, and growth.

When successful people are interviewed about the most influential people in their lives, a manager or boss is always in the top five. Surprising? It shouldn't be. Think of how impactful a manager really can be upon our experience at work.

As leadership consultants, we've had the privilege to spend many hours with executives discussing their talents, their teams, their challenges, and their goals. In the course of that time, we have heard some very moving stories. A few we will never forget, like this one:

This was during Desert Storm, and we were way out in the middle of nowhere, cut off from everything, and dug in. Dan, my boss, suddenly showed up out of nowhere. He grabbed me and helicoptered me to a transport back to the States, where Maria, my wife, was going into early labor.

It all turned out all right—with Maria—but the point is that Dan didn't just set things up for me, or call; he came himself and personally picked me up and made sure it happened. I don't know how. I think he gave me his ticket. And it wasn't just me that he helped; he was always doing something for the guys on our team. The guys, all of us, would still walk through a wall for Dan.

There are countless stories of these heroic managers, some not as dramatic perhaps, but no less significant to the people who tell the tales. We talk to people every day who have experienced powerful relationships with their supervisors and managers.

Americans spend the majority of our time at work; our livelihood depends upon it. Combine our dependence on work with the facts that organizational goals and strategies change continuously and are out of our immediate control, and you have a recipe for anxiety and stress.

Many stress tests note that getting a new manager is at the very top of the chart for situational stressors, second only to disasters like the loss of a spouse or job.

Our own research substantiates the importance of this particular perception with the item (survey question): *My manager really knows me.* When people feel that their manager knows them as a whole person— past, present, at work, and away from work—acceptance is felt and respect is communicated. The discovery of things in common, things that connect people, makes it easier to communicate and more likely that problems will be resolved, rather than escalated. Conversations lead to shared understanding, and shared understanding is the foundation for a relationship. Consider this example:

Recently, Jim, a friend of mine, was telling me about his job and some of the challenges he was facing. When I asked him about his manager, Jim really couldn't tell me much. He didn't know if his manager was married, single, or divorced, where he lived or has lived in the past, where he went to school, his career background, or anything about the man. Jim really didn't know him at all.

In our friend's case, many of the challenges Jim faced at work were related to the absence of a two-way relationship with his manager. His tendency to try new things, take risks, or go above and beyond the call of duty were greatly hampered by the lacking relationship.

Mutual trust and respect are the new motivators in the workplace.

People need to feel utilized and develop their talents to reach new levels of success.

Capability is essential for success. Consider star swimmer Michael Phelps, the most decorated Olympian of all time, having set 39 world records (the first at age 15).

What does Phelps have going for him? Consider just the physiological differences:

> Most people have a wingspan that matches their height. Not Phelps. He may be 6'4" tall, but his arms extend outward to a total of 6'7". The average shoe size for a person the size of Phelps is 12; he wears a size 14, which gives him an estimated 10% advantage over the competition.

> He also has a larger than average hand size which allows him to move more water.

> He has highly flexible knees and ankles, which act like flippers to literally propel him through the water.

> He has proportionately short legs (32 inch inseam) relative to his long, powerful trunk; this large upper body is the engine that powers his long arms. Moreover, his unique physique reduces drag through the water and allows for maximum propulsion.

> His muscles produce less lactic acid, meaning he can work at a higher capacity for longer periods with faster recovery.

A single one of these differences could give a swimmer an advantage; Michael has them all. Michael Phelps has more than just the physicality for greatness; he has the desire to perfect it.

He had the same great coach from age 11 and trained every day of the year, four hours in the pool and one hour on dry land. He perfected his stroke mechanics and focused his fiercely competitive nature.

Physiology, drive and discipline, they all combine to make Michael Phelps swim faster than 99% of other people.

What if our personal drive to win—our capability—is subverted by a culture that overlooks the individual?

Too often to count, cultures squander their talent. In 1972, the United Negro College Fund, in conjunction with the Ad Council, began a public awareness campaign that reflected this critical human need:

> The slogan, "A Mind is a Terrible Thing To Waste," has remained unchanged for more than three decades and has become part of the American vernacular.[12]

The American public responded by donating $2.2 billion dollars to help more than 350,000 minority students graduate. The UNCF 's roster of celebrity supporters includes John F. Kennedy, Maya Angelou, Chairman of the Joint Chiefs of Staff Colin Powell and his wife Alma, Michael Jordan, and Spike Lee—all of whom have contributed their own considerable talent to its mission.

Have you ever felt as if your day were wasted at work?

One of the universal needs that propel humans is the need to *feel useful*. Our sense of self-worth, pride, and confidence are driven and developed by the degree to which we feel our personal talents and abilities are being utilized.

We are all born with the potential for excellence. Our MicroCultures (first family, then school groups, and then work units) provide an opportunity to use our unique gifts to reach unprecedented levels of performance.

Yet we often encounter people who haven't figured out how and where to invest their unique talents. It is not always easy, and the MacroCulture's obsession with *weakness prevention* distorts the process and confuses the priorities. It has us scrambling to *fix* everything, from bad breath and shyness to premature balding.

The self-help section of bookstores and download sites are overflowing with the kind of advice that leads to self-doubt and myopic superficiality.

The natural variation of the human condition is a vital part of its beauty and strength.

Have you spent time really trying to identify your own talents, strengths, capabilities, and inspirations? What do you do better than 97 percent of other people?

Unfortunately, people are often blind to their own talents. They can't always explain how they do what they do and rarely delineate their talents and capabilities in detail. It can be difficult for them to acknowledge their excellence and see their unique, highly individualized gifts.

We need others to help us in that process, to *hold up a mirror*, so to speak. That is one of the distinguishing characteristics of the world's greatest managers (and teachers).[13]

Once discovered, people want to use their gifts; there is nothing worse than spending a day in a role that leaves you feeling bored, tired, and underutilized. Unfortunately, people get stuck in positions that don't fit their talents or inclinations, and it's difficult for them to get out. They begin to look defective if they do the wrong tasks long enough.

When the talent doesn't fit the expectations, individuals are slow to learn, and the challenge is more defeating than inspiring. This works against the person's development and often puts him or her further behind the curve.

In many cases, the individual is forced to seek a venue for the expression of his or her talent outside the organization. Many communities, schools, and churches are the beneficiaries of talents not well utilized at work as people with a yearning to express their gifts search for meaningful opportunities.

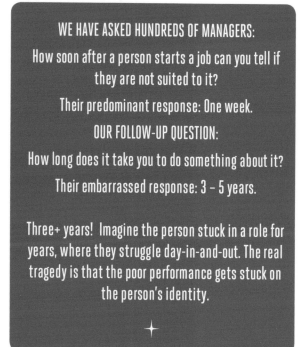

WE HAVE ASKED HUNDREDS OF MANAGERS:

How soon after a person starts a job can you tell if they are not suited to it?

Their predominant response: One week.

OUR FOLLOW-UP QUESTION:

How long does it take you to do something about it?

Their embarrassed response: 3 – 5 years.

Three+ years! Imagine the person stuck in a role for years, where they struggle day-in-and-out. The real tragedy is that the poor performance gets stuck on the person's identity.

Loss of fit to one's work is like a small death. The first stage is denial and later the anger sets in.

If we don't seek others to challenge us and coach us to full impact, we can end up bitter and even envious of exceptional performance in others.

Feeling underutilized is often one of the first signs of disengagement, and left untended for many years, people can become *actively dis-engaged*. It's important to recognize that these are *states of being* and not *traits* of engagement, but the underlying causes can be so systemic that change is virtually impossible.

Energy is abundant when strength is accentuated.

Practice will always be essential for greatness, but the process itself is intrinsically rewarding as the person evolves, testing themselves and reaching unprecedented levels of performance. Like Michael Phelps, if we use our strengths, we can recover faster and increase our capability with renewed energy.

Vital MicroCultures display a collective passion for improvement. Feeling one's gifts are being fully utilized is one of the most powerful forces in driving sustainable engagement at work, home, and in our communities.

+ + +

LOST CONNECTION HOW PEOPLE DISCONNECT FROM CULTURE.

When our nearest and dearest cultures begin to change, it rocks our world. That's why organizational change is so difficult for the people within—they fall out of control and the change is taking place in their *nest*, where they spend the majority of their time. It is no wonder that the reaction is often far more emotional than rational.

There are three ways that people disconnect from an organizational culture:

- *We can be terminated (fired, not assassinated).*
- *We can quit and leave.*
- *We can quit and stay.*

Each scenario leaves its mark on the individual and the culture.

When individuals are dismissed from a culture they cherished, they display all kinds of stress associated with that loss. We have seen dramatic, even violent, situations that reflect the culture's importance to those people.

A faculty member loses tenure and turns to violence.

A long-term employee is laid off and verbally attacks the manager and team responsible.

A lonely teen acts out his frustrations on the cliques that excluded him.

When individuals make the decision to quit and leave, they could be optimistic, headed toward greener pastures, or they could be running for the hills with their tails between their legs to escape a culture that didn't fit.

The final way we disconnect from a culture is the most common of the three: quitting and staying. We stay inside the formal lines, but the culture has lost its power to motivate, inspire, or create growth within us.

LOSING AN ICON
A culture often mourns the loss of a special person who was revered by its members. These icons can stay in our collective memory for a very long time:

Elvis Presley, Martin Luther King, John Lennon, John F. Kennedy, and Marilyn Monroe.

- *We live in the neighborhood, but shut the garage door before we get out of our cars.*

- *We pay our dues, but don't attend the meetings or functions, never help with the goals or share in the purpose.*

- *We come to work from nine to five, do the minimum to get our check, and save our passion for five to nine.*

We will take a closer look at the challenges associated with the people who quit and stay, those we call the *Actively Dis-engaged*.

+ + +

CAVE DWELLERS CONSISTENTLY AGAINST VIRTUALLY EVERYTHING

Our research with the Actively Dis-engaged has revealed some important distinctions. The data suggests a full 35 percent of the workforce is Actively Dis-engaged. These are individuals we sometimes refer to as CAVE dwellers, *Consistently Against Virtually Everything*!

No matter what percentage of your overall workforce is actively dis-engaged, we find that the following explanations hold true:

- *Some of the Actively Dis-engaged came this way;*

- *Some aren't really a fit for their role;*

- *Some hate feeling this way, but are stuck; or*

- *Maybe it's the manager?*

The percentage of Actively Dis-engaged reflects the unique circumstances of each specific person, team, and manager. What you should do about the Actively Dis-engaged depends on *why* these people are so disconnected. Let's take a look at each option from the perspective of the person.

Reason #1: They Came This Way

A certain percentage of the Actively Dis-engaged came that way into your organization or team. You didn't grow them, you selected them. Maybe you liked their educational profile or prior work experience? Perhaps they were particularly verbal or engaging during the interview process?

Whatever the reason, you hired yourself an individual who resists belonging and then makes it your fault. You can't change the individual's personality or anti-everything theme. At the very least, be happy that you did not marry them!

What should you do about it?

Managers tell us it takes mere days to know if a new hire really fits the organization or the work. Unfortunately, it often takes 3 – 5 years to do something about it.

Don't let that statistic be you! Act quickly and probe the person about the role. Is it meeting the individual's expectations? Is the individual meeting yours? By not allowing the employee to languish in a poor fit, you're ensuring a brighter future for everybody involved.

Consider this example offered by Jane, a leader we know who knows the value of acting quickly when the "fit" between the person and the role isn't right:

> We get quite a few referrals of new hires from employees we have terminated because we make sure we respect the dignity of the person who is leaving the position. I want to feel that if I run into an ex-employee at Target, we can say hello and not feel uncomfortable around one another...
>
> As a result, we have received many new-hire referrals from ex-employees. They'll tell their friends, "Look, it wasn't right for me, but I think you'd love working there."

This might explain why this organization's employee attrition rate is only one-fourth that of other health care providers, and they have few problems recruiting.

Reason #2: They're Not Really a Fit for the Role

A certain number of your Actively Dis-engaged don't *fit* their job. Maybe early in their career, they fit, but changes in the expectations or a promotion have rendered them incapable of excelling at their current role. They face challenges for which there is no response in their repertoire. This is a miserable experience for both the individual and the organization.

Research with the Actively Dis-engaged suggests that they are, on average, using less than 22 percent of their unique capabilities at work. They are exhausted emotionally and physically by work that simply doesn't fit who they are.

If the job doesn't fit, poor performance will follow.

They are likely to experience a renewed sense of engagement *only* if they can be *recast* into another role—or enabled to find one elsewhere.

Step in to see if the person can be recast in another role or one with a slightly different focus and expectations. If there is nothing for which the person is well suited, this could be a time to utilize your performance improvement process. Make the standards clear so that the person knows the level of accomplishment they must achieve to continue in the role.

Reason #3: They Hate Feeling This Way, but They Are Stuck

A certain percent of your Actively Dis-engaged actually hate feeling that way much more than you dislike having them actively dis-engaged. They feel completely out of sync with the organization and with their relationships in it, including the one they have with you—their manager or co-worker.

Sometimes highly talented and motivated people just get crossways with the organization and find it exceedingly difficult to find their way back to engagement.

People who are miserable and hate being actively dis-engaged are easier to spot. They are often crying out or acting out. They will have friends who care about them and are supporting them; these friends know they feel *disenfranchised* rather than dis-engaged.

What can be done about it?

Help these people to take on or own something so they can begin to see the value of their contributions. If you sincerely can't make that effort, perhaps there are other opportunities within the organization where these people can make a fresh start.

A new manager who sees the talent of the individual and is committed to developing a relationship with the person can regenerate engagement. Long-term employees may benefit from this kind of intensive resuscitation to reconnect with their work and their organization.

Reason #4: Maybe It's the Manager

A certain percentage of the Actively Dis-engaged group results from a manager who cannot create a sense of future, purpose, or value within the individual. These individuals are so mismanaged and overlooked that unless the manager is changed out, the organization may permanently lose their talent.

When groups are chronically Actively Dis-engaged, it might be time to recast the manager into a non-managerial role. Like everyone else, fit is critical. Effective managers start the year with the team they are given, but they end the year with the team they deserve.

+ + +

RIDING THE BUS TO EXCELLENCE
FINDING PURPOSE MEANS DISCOVERING LINE-OF-SIGHT.

Just get through it. That was our predominant thought when returning a rental car and boarding the shuttle to the airport. We had the vacation, having experienced some of the best dining and shopping venues of Scottsdale, and now we were headed home. We didn't expect to feel like guests on a shuttle, and we certainly didn't expect Johnny-Jay—the most engaged shuttle driver in Phoenix—to wow us with his service.

I realized he was different from the first moment he addressed me— smiling with delight, his arms wide open—the way you greet an old friend. The other passengers quickly hurled their baggage and strollers into the gut of the shuttle, as if at any moment the doors might slam shut and separate them from their belongings.

But Johnny-Jay insisted I drop my roller bag, tucked my briefcase to his side, and led me to a standing post right behind his seat. He placed my briefcase behind his chair, reassured me that he would take care of everything, and strode back into the mob of passengers to dispense calm, assistance, and welcome.

Yes, it was great service, but it was only the beginning of the *experience.*

We discovered that Johnny has been officially named as the *number one driver in Phoenix,* and I think it would be fair to say *the world,* and we counted ourselves among the lucky to be traveling to Terminal 3 with him as our chauffeur.[14]

Johnny has some fun with his title. We passed a colleague of his driving in the opposite direction, and Johnny pointed her out, indicating that she wasn't number one. In Johnny's own words, "She's my friend, but she can be very unfriendly." The bus roared; don't we all know somebody like Johnny's friend?

> ### SERVANT VERSUS SERVITUDE
>
> Does service to others enrich you – or demean you
>
> When people love to be of service to others, they are servant leaders – taking pride in the contribution they make.
>
> When that role is not a fit, the position feels like servitude – being placed in indentured service against your will.

And don't we all know what it feels like to be waited on by an "indentured servant?"

The mayor, among others, has interviewed Johnny to discover how he came to be named the number one driver by so many people. Johnny makes it seem—*duh*—so obvious:

> This bus is my home, and I treat my passengers like I treat guests in my own home.

Johnny reveres his guests. He openly acknowledges that we—his passengers—could have visited anywhere and yet came to the Phoenix area. In the process, as Johnny points out, we left a lot of our money in the city, money that the local economy really needs. He appreciates what our patronage does beyond the dollars—jobs for him and his family and funding for schools, parks, and streets.

WHAT EACH PERSON SHOULD EXPECT FROM WORK:

- To be genuinely appreciated.
- To have work that really "fits" your talents and expectations.
- To have the opportunity to help people - your customers and your team.
- To see the real outcomes of your work - why you do what you do.
- To achieve excellence - to be successful.
- To see the unique value you bring to the organization.
- To grow in your own skills and abilities.
- To have fun at work.
- To be trusted.
- To be able to trust.

It was not just what Johnny said, but how his passengers felt. On Johnny-Jay's bus, we felt *valued.*

He confided that he once left his shuttle to drive a city bus but quit just two days later. We asked him what took him so long. His reply:

> That's not a culture I can live in.

Johnny-Jay gave us a lot to think about that Saturday morning. As long-time consultants in talent, engagement, and culture, we revisited our fundamental beliefs and research roots through one man's amazing expression of his own individual gifts, his line-of-sight to his customers, and his ability to perform his role at a whole new level.

LEAVING HOPELESS AND VICTIM HEADING FOR CONFIDENT AND COMMITTED.

Imagine how much more clear work would be if we had individual *sensors* that visibly showed how engaged we were. *Look at me, my light is green today! Golly, I'm feeling productive!*

Alternatively: *Uh-oh, my sensor is beeping and the light is red...Oh no, here comes the boss! Can anybody lend me a green Skittle?*

Admittedly, it would be highly distracting to see the flashing red light on the forehead of the person packing your parachute or the surgeon performing your surgery. Imagine seeing the actual engagement level of the person maintaining the hydraulic system while your daughter is boarding the helicopter!

If these imaginary sensors were in place, our cultures would improve because there's nothing like facing the truth to make people more practical. And the truth is: When somebody isn't engaged with his or her activity— whatever that may be—everybody else suffers. So how do people get so far down the path of disengagement?

The typical business garb includes glistening golden handcuffs: a steady, healthy paycheck, medical insurance for the family, high unemployment to inspire fear, and ten years of time invested. The list goes on. These are the *rational* reasons we hold on to a situation that's flashing red.

> *In these instances, you can literally feel your self-concept dialing 911. "Hello, dispatch? You've got to help me. I'm in deep and I need to—" Beeeeeeeeeep.*

The dial tone is the sound of your mind silencing your soul.

What are the risks to the individual (her growth, engagement, effectiveness) from remaining in a role that silences the spirit?

If we keep silent about this condition, nobody will know what we're going through, and nobody will be able to help. We are all highly dependent upon others to hold up a mirror to our lives and our work and help us reach excellence. This mirror helps us to better appreciate our contributions and our strengths.

The MicroCulture is most affected by the people who belong to it. Rather than operate as victims of our culture, we own a *time-share* within it— every day when we arrive.

Hanging on to resentment is like taking poison and expecting someone else to die.

What happens when we feel this way?

Imagine if 40 percent of a third-grader's waking hours were invested with a teacher whose personal connection to that child and that classroom is color-coded red—"actively dis-engaged".

What is the cumulative affect of a poor teacher on a single high-risk child? The entire year becomes a lesson in what a child cannot do.

Now imagine that it's your child in that classroom, twiddling her thumbs.

It's the teachers who care that hold students accountable and inspire a leap to a new level of growth. Potential is universal—we all have it—and it's tragic for the entire human community when that potential isn't fully realized.

+

When we feel discouraged, negative, unappreciated, dis-engaged, angry, we tend to share those emotions with others around us.

Unfortunately, the more we dwell on our negative emotions, the more negative we become and the more entrenched in the problem.

Some people enable us; they listen, but cosign our negative feelings and keep us stuck in the problem.

People can help us, but it depends on the person. Others can help us move past the problem, gain traction on a positive path.

THE 3 MOST PARALYZING WORDS

- Don't

- Won't

- Can't

These 4-letter words freeze forward movement.

+

Fundamentally, we each must take stock of our own reactions to the work environment. Are we viewing ourselves as victims or owners of the cultures to which we belong? The former view truncates our talent and initiative while the latter helps us shape the circumstances more to our own liking.

+   +   +

TRANSITIONING FROM VICTIM TO OWNER

Recognize that you have the right stuff (energy, talent, and drive) to make a difference in your culture.

Every day there are hundreds of moments—touchpoints—in which you either add or detract energy from those around you (your team, your manager, your customer). Make a conscious decision to contribute.

Review what you can take ownership of—what's your role? What are healthy options you can take?

SUMMARY: WHAT PEOPLE REALLY NEED FROM THEIR MICROCULTURE

A culture's energy comes from the people within and their level of engagement in the MicroCulture. The individual is the ultimate test for understanding the real impact of culture on performance; does each person:

1) Know the real outcomes and true purpose of work?
2) Have trusting and supportive relationships with others?
3) Have the opportunity to utilize and grow his or her talent and capability?

Does the culture invite individual growth, creativity, and service, *or* does it inhibit energy and stifle passion?

In spite of our efforts to improve performance, most organizations struggle to provide what people really need most to be successful— an emotional connection to the team and the work.

In the following section, we'll focus our attention on the interconnectivity between MicroCultures and the role managers and leaders play in connecting their people with purpose to bring out the passion within.

+   +   +

Section Three

BRIDGECULTURE: CONNECTING PEOPLE TO PURPOSE
LINE-OF-SIGHT IS THE BRIDGE.

The flight was late and so was the hour. I rushed from Terminal A6 to Terminal C33 to make my second connecting flight in what had become a Homeric journey from Minneapolis. If I missed the flight, I would also miss the next flight, and I wouldn't be able to make it home.

When I finally arrived at my gate, the agents told me good news: The incoming aircraft just landed and would be departing shortly. I took a deep breath and found a seat in the terminal.

A few minutes later, I heard my name paged and reported back to the desk. "We are so sorry," the agent explained. "We just realized that you were on the San Luis Obispo flight out of LA, and there's not enough time for you to make the connection. But we've done some checking, and there's a direct flight to San Luis Obispo leaving in twenty minutes. We are going to get you on that direct flight—and you can skip LA altogether."

"Bless you!" I said. This, for me, was a first. As a frequent flyer, rarely had I seen such initiative and concern take place in an airport. Unfortunately, my journey had just begun...

Excellence is never the result of just performing a task. Excellence comes from connecting the tasks we perform to a deeply felt purpose.

As we saw in the MicroCulture, individuals who have a clear line-of-sight to their customer (Johnny-Jay, the bus driver, for example) feel a stronger sense of satisfaction and fulfillment from seeing the real outcomes of their work. In the case above, the agent's primary focus was to ensure her customer made it home that night.

One agent ordered a cart to ferry me to the next terminal and assured me that I would make the gate in time, while the other agent called ahead to the gate to make sure that the flight was being held.

I watched the agent dial again and again, attempting to reach the San Luis Obispo gate attendants for the new flight. When her numerous calls went unanswered, the agent became frustrated and decided that she must take stronger action. She called a friendly colleague at a nearby gate and requested the friend run and physically hold the San Luis Obispo flight for me.

Individual efforts are only part of the story of organizational excellence. Especially difficult outcomes are often beyond the reach of individual players and require teamwork and collaboration. The heroes in the above example set the standard for organizational excellence when they called their extended corporate family to deliver the customer's goals.

I felt relieved, impressed, and re-energized by the responsiveness of these two women; other passengers around the gate watched this "above and beyond" level of service as it unfolded.

The other passengers looked at me as though I were someone important. Right at that moment, I, too, believed that I was important.

At some point, every one of us has experienced exemplary service that delivers the organization's promise—its brand. It makes us feel valued and honored by the people who help us. This level of service builds an intense sense of loyalty and belief in the brand promise. In this case, *friendly skies.*

Billions of dollars are invested in brand each year—all with the hope this strategy will increase market share by acquiring and retaining customers.

Unfortunately, brand only makes the promise. It is the culture that either fulfills these promises...or breaks them.

Halfway down the terminal—riding in the back of the cart—I heard my name again over the PA. Uh-oh. Hope fizzled as I asked the driver to turn the cart around.

The two agents looked as disappointed as I felt inside. "The San Luis Obispo gate attendants closed the Jetway," one woman said regretfully. In spite of everything...

For the San Luis Obispo gate attendants, it was nothing personal, just business as usual, standard operating procedure. Customers come and go all day;

> "No" is an easy answer.
>
> It is programmed into our policies, procedures and other work structures.
>
> "Yes" requires human energy to make things happen.
>
> ✦

why hold the gate for an unknown customer? There will be another flight tomorrow.

What happens to the hopes and expectations of top performers when the culture surrounding them fails to live up to their standards? When the policies, procedures, and service partners are obstacles to outstanding performance? What happens to the customer's belief in the brand when the organization fails to deliver the promised outcome?

Brand promise exposes the organization's highest expectations for performance. To achieve it, the culture must reflect the brand.

These are the issues inherent within the BridgeCulture. The BridgeCulture is the connective tissue uniting our MicroCultures to one another and to the organization's mission and purpose. Functioning like an air-traffic control center, effective BridgeCultures coordinate the organization's groups to deliver exemplary service. This means the culture must compliment the brand.

People within organizations connect hundreds of times each day to deliver services, products, and support for the mission and goals. These connecting points are opportunities for either inspired partnership or dashed hopes. Are you building bridges or burning them? Is the focus on the customer or on internal policies and procedures?

Does the culture fortify the brand?

+ + +

BRAND AND CULTURE: ORGANIZATIONAL COUSINS?

Advertising exemplifies the relationship between emotion and brand. Products are always advertised via a human/emotional connection. When products are campaigned with celebrity endorsement, consumers relate to the celebrities more than the products. *Bill Murray uses this deodorant; am I the sort of person who uses the same deodorant as Bill Murray? Yes. Wanda Sykes? Maybe. Dr. Phil? No thanks.*

Consider the *Most Interesting Man in the World*:

> *He wouldn't be afraid to show his feminine side...if he had one.*
> *His mother has a tattoo that reads "Son."*
> *At museums, he's allowed to touch the art.*

He's the most interesting man in the world.
"I don't always drink beer, but when I do I prefer Dos Equis." [15]

In another cult-inspiring advertising glimpse, **HE** sits silently with a gentle, penetrating machismo (silence speaks volumes) as two gorgeous women (they are always gorgeous) discuss the tween sensation vampire-film series *Twilight*. He slowly turns to the camera and states, "I have no idea what this means..."

We love him, that mysterious, sophisticated, ever-cool, white-jacket-wearing hero, and he is a completely contrived individual that we channel when we drink the beer. Men want to be him and women simply want him. It's about *being* the most interesting man in the world.

Brand is not about the product; it's about our emotional connection to the product.

What is the difference between brand and culture?

Brand is how others see us. Culture is how we see ourselves.

Take a look at these three brand principles:

1) Brand is always evolving; either you manage that evolution or you don't.
2) The definition of the brand rests in the mind of the customer.
3) Brand is a union of rational with emotional.

Brand and culture are kindred organizational spirits. For both brand and culture, the same qualities apply—alive, always evolving—and for both, the impact lies in the eye of the beholder (customer or employee).

For optimal impact, the culture must align with the brand or risk a disconnection between the promise and the delivery.

One could argue that if the Most Interesting Man in the World were a real person, the danger would be discovering his foibles. *Did he really nod off after dinner? Did he need to describe his entire round of golf, hole after hole, stroke after stroke? He's acting like a mere mortal!*

A misaligned culture can crash an entire franchise. One of the longest-running and most successful television sitcoms of all time, *Two and a Half Men*, fell to earth when its already controversial star, Charlie Sheen, completely left the rails of reason and showered contempt on the brand.[16]

The true sin was that the controversy brought reality crashing into our emotional fantasy. Similarly to the most interesting man in the world, the public coveted the make-believe Charlie, who dared to dangle over the edge of morality and proper behavior but always landed on his feet with a laugh track. Sheen's train wreck burst the brand's magic, which depended upon escaping reality, not wallowing in it.

Hollywood stars create their own brands and continuously manage the emotional connection with their followers. Some are masters, and others end up hawking skin care products on late-night television, but they all function in the fickle and fleeting connection between brand and culture.

+ + +

BRAND CREATES A DESIRE TO BELONG
CULTURE CEMENTS THE RELATIONSHIP.

The more powerful and emotional the brand promise, the greater the dependence on the culture to deliver.

Take luxury brands, for example, organizations like the Ritz-Carlton. Their motto: "Ladies and gentlemen serving ladies and gentlemen." The organization acknowledges that the experience of the guest is more than just luxurious amenities. An emotional connection is therefore required in the following circumstances:

The booking process
Arrival at the hotel
The check-in experience
Porter's service
Concierge's savvy
Maid service
Room service

Each connection presents an opportunity to fulfill, disappoint, or exceed the expectations of the guest. The gap between the guest's expectations and the guest's experience may close or widen; with each experience, the brand promise is further shaped for better or worse:

During our first visit to the hotel, our room was an absolute delight. It overlooked the lake, and my wife, Jane, and I had breakfast in bed for the first time since our kids were born; the concierge had arranged a special arrival package of truffles and wine. It was simply perfect. It was as if they knew us.

> *When Jane and I returned on our next anniversary, it was a serious disappointment. The staff just seemed to go through the motions. It wasn't terrible, but...*

Our experiences become the standard against which other services are measured. If that experience is exemplary, the bar goes up.

This happens in every industry. It is a fact of life; organizations fail with some of their most valuable customers not because they deliver poorly, but because their service is inconsistent. Consider this customer's experience:

> *Gina, our favorite waitress, always finds us a great table near the window and gets our coffee before we even get settled; she knows we like to sit a bit before we order.*

> *When Gina isn't here, it is just not the same place. If we know she's not working, we go somewhere else.*

From the customer's perspective, the server *is* the organization. When that employee leaves, when our favorite server is on her lunch break, when the technician who helped us last time isn't available, as customers, we prepare to be disappointed, because we usually are.

Inconsistencies are the bane of leadership's existence.

In response, leaders often seek a scalable solution. They try training and scripting to "bottle up" their best service and deliver it consistently. Unfortunately, what is charming and engaging from one person may seem contrived and artificial from another; a scripted voice sounds lifeless and false enthusiasm feels alienating.

When we understand that the inconsistency is symptomatic of a larger issue—namely the emotional connection between the server and the customer—it becomes apparent that this connection *can't* be scripted. Rather, it is the domain of a clear line-of-sight and an authentic, emotional connection.

A waitress, nurse, salesman, clerk, or accountant with an excellent line-of-sight to the customer will engage that customer in ways that communicate his or her appreciation for the customer's needs, outcomes, and concerns. In extending themselves to the customer, these people create an emotional connection that improves both sides of the equation. They cannot be scripted to connect because their customer is unique, and so are they.

When we study excellence in any role, we are amazed at its many facets.

Outstanding players are as unique from one another as they are disparate from their more average coworkers. Their individual style, language, and personality shine through their work and render them both memorable and genuine from the customer's perspective.

Talented people with line-of-sight to the customer are critical for competitive advantage.

There is no substitute for the way they partner together - embracing customer needs to deliver exemplary results.

When human beings come up against business framework, a bridge is either built or fractured. Effective BridgeCultures encourage people to connect in a way that brings life and legitimacy to the brand promise in the mind of the customer; it wraps around the business of the business, aligning people with purpose.

The following three elements can become either opportunities for alignment or barriers to performance:

1) The structures that define our function.

   Organizational structure defines how we relate to one another. But the very structures that divide people into separate departments, teams, or groups can fracture our efforts to collaborate or communicate. Silos and turf wars can erupt, reinforcing an us-versus-them mentality that creates barriers to innovation, service, and performance.

2) The management and leadership that connect the people.

   We are all a part of the BridgeCulture, but managers and supervisors are the primary translators. They set the stage for connections, interpret policies and processes for people, and create or eliminate barriers. The best managers are connectors more than controllers, using their touchpoints with people to focus talent and energy on the organization's true purpose: service to the customer.

3) The purpose that unites and inspires us.

   At its best, the BridgeCulture supports the brand promise. It is built on line-of-sight with the customer, the ultimate North Star of organizational effectiveness. When every employee and every team has a clear line-of-sight, decisions and actions are focused on acquiring and retaining customers, the key to organic growth.

THE LITTLE BOXES THAT DIVIDE US JOB DESCRIPTIONS (AND OTHER MYTHICAL BEASTS OF ORGANIZATIONAL DESIGN) MEET HUMAN COMPLEXITY.

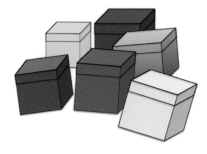

The organizational chart is a framework around which the organization's culture grows. Therein are reflected the various groups, roles, and responsibilities which represent the business of the business—on paper. It is the rational explanation for how things work together—as opposed to the way they really work. As people interact with the formal work structures, both Micro- and BridgeCultures take shape.

As we have discussed, people are "messy," and they often do not bear much resemblance to the job descriptions of their position. It is not that most are incapable of delivering what is expected; it is that a generic job description isn't a very good fit for an actual living human being!

We Don't Understand Culture Until We Understand How the Rational Affects the Emotional

THE RATIONAL ASPECTS OF ORGANIZATIONS

Job Descriptions

Hierarchy

Process & Procedures

Rules

Plans

THE EMOTIONAL ELEMENTS

Talent – what people do best

Trust

Creativity

Service

Innovation

Organizational charts, job descriptions, and performance evaluations put us in "little boxes" that belie our inherent individuality.

So in practice, job descriptions are a laundry list of tasks and activities that provide an approximate estimate of the nature of a role and hopefully link to some positive and desired outcomes. Let's not take these "little boxes" too seriously.

A generic job description is like wearing someone else's clothes: the neck may be too tight, the sleeves too long, and the style just doesn't fit—no matter how long you wear it.

Consider that no two people are exactly alike. The closer you come to a real person, the more he or she defies classification.

A person has a nearly limitless range of emotions, motivations, relationships, and contradictions. For each individual, the best opportunity for success is in a role that fits that person's unique set of needs, talents, and capabilities. Decades of research continues to support the importance of this to individual energy and performance.[17]

That said, the best managers create better energy and performance by adjusting responsibilities to the individual's strengths and capabilities.

Great managers translate the basic expectations of the role into the right expectations for the person and the team.

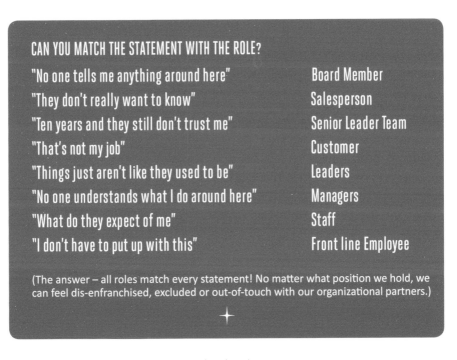

CAN YOU MATCH THE STATEMENT WITH THE ROLE?

"No one tells me anything around here"	Board Member
"They don't really want to know"	Salesperson
"Ten years and they still don't trust me"	Senior Leader Team
"That's not my job"	Customer
"Things just aren't like they used to be"	Leaders
"No one understands what I do around here"	Managers
"What do they expect of me"	Staff
"I don't have to put up with this"	Front line Employee

(The answer – all roles match every statement! No matter what position we hold, we can feel dis-enfranchised, excluded or out-of-touch with our organizational partners.)

BRIDGING THE CONTINENTAL DIVIDE STAFF AND LINE.

The boxes on the organizational chart do more than provide definition to our actions within MicroCultures and the immediate team, they carry enormous implications for cross-organizational synergy.

> *The distinction between staff and line is reminiscent of the Continental Divide.*
>
> *It may be crossed, but the majority of people just stand on the precipice and offer armchair observations of the opposing cliff.*

The further removed from the line, the more likely a group's performance is based on perception, rather than hard, measurable indicators. In a typical office or staff environment, maximum attention is placed on supervisor approval and minimum attention on performance outcomes (as they likely do not exist).

Staff attempts to provide objective measures frequently rely upon the line management to "find the time" for activities the line views as administrative and impractical. The subsequent reports are not true outcomes but activity measures (i.e., the number of managers having completed and filed action plans, the number of managers through manager development training, or completed performance reviews). This naturally creates tension between line and staff.

Outstanding staff have the ability to leap the great divide and often see themselves as a "servant" to the field, rather than as a teacher, coach, or conscience.

The VP of HR in a manufacturing organization described her experience:

> *I make it a practice to visit each department to both understand their issues and to connect to the real purpose of the work. I never cease to be amazed at their reactions.*

> *One production manager, Hector, said: "Can you please stop by our local HR department before you leave and tell them what you were doing here? They never visit our business unit."*

Being a great servant to the line organization means being interested in the line's goals and issues, not a missionary on a quest of one's own making.

Beyond line and staff, there are divisions, departments, and teams. These structural definitions threaten to separate us into different "tribes." To truly meet and exceed our goals requires synergy, partnership, and innovation.

Managers and leaders are keepers of the bridge; they set the stage, whether it be for collaboration or competition. Some create silos that are reinforced by their own people, and others encourage their people to reach out and connect with service partners.

When people interact with the structure of the organization, the situation offers an opportunity for heroes, politicians or victims to emerge.

The effectiveness of the BridgeCulture depends on the proportion of this mix within the organization, and that depends on the primary connectors within: managers and leaders.

Do they:

- Use structure as a guide rather than a rule book?
- Consistently prioritize people over process in a way that maximizes performance?
- Set the stage for their people to cross-connect and form relationships with their service partners?

+   +   +

A CASE OF BROKEN PROMISES
WHEN THE BRIDGECULTURE FRACTURES.

Below is an actual online chat between a customer and a "Zzion" representative.

Alicia: Welcome to Zzion online sales support! What services may I help you learn more about today?

Customer: I have the highest speed Internet you offer, and it is still so slow my videos stop about four times a minute. Can you help?

Alicia: Thank you for being a valued Zzion customer. I would be more than happy to assist you with your services.

Alicia: There are a number of factors that influence speed, including the condition of your telephone line, the wiring inside your location, the amount of congestion on the Internet itself, and the speed of the websites or servers that you connect to on the Internet. For all these reasons, the actual connection and throughput speeds of the service are not guaranteed.

Customer: That's really helpful.

Alicia: Is FIRO available to you?

Customer: I took the highest speed offered when I switched my service. I am not sure if that was FIRO.

Alicia: Let me send you a link to check to see if FIRO is available to you.

Customer: I just checked my bill. I am being charged for FIRO Double Play, which includes FIRO Internet 25/15 for $89.99 per month.

Alicia: Do you have the option to upgrade your Internet speed?

Customer: Are you telling me that this speed is your FIRO? This is slower than the service I switched from. I was told this would be faster.

Alicia: Speed varies by location.

Alicia: I can send you a link to do a speed test.

Alicia: Would you like me to send you the link?

Customer: Yes. Please.

Alicia: Please click here for the speed test.

After the speed test is performed, a page of results is provided and the conversation continues.

Customer: 7.69 mbps download; 8.29 mbps upload. I got a page of results and then the site did not respond to a request and the network browser got tired of waiting for a reply and stopped.

Customer: Is that the speed I am paying for?

Alicia: Unfortunately, I don't have access to your account information. I recommend you call customer care and they will be able to assist you further.

Alicia: Would you like for me to send you the number?

Customer: Why is the speed 7.69/8.29 and not 25/15?

Alicia: Unfortunately, I don't have information on that.

Alicia: I have not heard from you for a few moments. Would you like to continue this chat session?

Customer: My fingers are speechless. Please send the customer care number and I will see if they are able to assist me further.

Alicia: You may call the local Zzion business office between 8:00AM and 6:00PM EST from Monday to Friday.

Alicia: Can I assist you with anything further today?

Customer: I don't want to take up too much of your time.

Alicia: You're welcome. It was my pleasure assisting you today. If you have any additional questions, please do not hesitate to contact us again. Have a nice day.

Your chat session has been terminated by the Zzion chat representative.

How did that interaction make you feel? Alicia is "programmed" to respond to questions of speed, so she was ready for this; she probably gets this question all the time. Let's identify the responses that feel scripted or dictated by the organization:

Alicia: Is FIRO available to you?

She is ready to up-sell FIRO at the drop of a hat. Is she in customer service or sales? *Both?* Her next move: provide a speed test link. However, it's not part of her job to interpret the results of that test in relation to the package the customer is actually paying for monthly. From the customer's standpoint, that's a huge disconnect. If you recommend a test and know a customer's package, it seems like a chat representative should comment on the comparison.

At every juncture, Alicia's response tosses the ball back in the customer's court. It is the customer's job:

- *To log in*
- *To know what FIRO means*
- *To figure out the source of interference*
- *To run the speed test*
- *To interpret the speed test*
- *To call customer care if they are persistent or curious enough to care what the test means in relation to service for which they have already paid*

It is always the customer's problem. If it were Zzion's problem, there would be much more interest in solving it. At some point, however, it actually *will* become Zzion's problem: to retain their customer.

The conversation creates angst, a wishing that Alicia would be free to respond as a fellow human being. Couldn't she recognize the inherent disconnect from being sold the "fastest Internet available" and then to subsequently experience service that makes cable companies look good?

> *She said she would be pleased to have the customer contact her again... why does that seem unbelievable? That statement seemed false and made us question whether she had ever intended to help.*

> *If they sold us high-speed Internet, the Internet better be high-speed! If it's not, then what are we all doing here? Get somebody out here, somebody who knows what 25/15 means, and figure this thing out!*

Anticipating customer needs is not necessarily bad, but doing it for the company's purpose rather than the customer's purpose makes the whole process go haywire.

It is the equivalent of telling someone what they mean rather than attempting to understand them.

What if Alicia thought the primary purpose of her role was acquiring and retaining customers? How differently might she have responded?

+ + +

YOU CAN'T GET THERE FROM HERE
WEAKNESS PREVENTION ≠ EXCELLENCE PROMOTION.

When sales are slow and times are tough, we have a tendency to take our eyes off the top line and look for ways to shrink our organizations into prosperity by lowering costs.

Much of our organizational energy has been directed to what can best be termed "weakness prevention"—the elimination of defects. Programs like Six Sigma, Lean, and Kaizen have made timeless contributions and proven invaluable to organizations. They affect the culture in many positive ways and contribute to our ability to assess results relative to quality.

> Why have we seen so many initiatives (Six Sigma, LEAN, etc) to manage costs?
>
> The obvious answer is to improve quality, reduce errors, eliminate waste and create customer trust.
>
> But, is that entirely honest? Or has it been more about managing costs in order to show earnings when sales go flat or decline?

Organizations experiencing problems with product/service/quality typically work to implement solutions based on these programs and "acculturate" them into the organization. And that's when we're called—in the *aftermath.*

Minimizing defects is just fine, but it doesn't produce *excellence*, the superior end result. Suggesting that excellence is simply the absence of defects is like saying:

Perfect pitch, cadence, and tone make a person an American Idol.

A high GPA makes one a Rhodes scholar.

Perfect punctuation is John Grisham's secret to success

There is an emotional dimension to excellence that carries more influence than a mere absence of error.

Organizations are in a struggle for dominion in a world where *the emotional connection* counts far more than *the rational* in gaining and maintaining market share. It is a place where the minimization of defects is necessary but not sufficient to achieve the *real* outcomes desired.

Minimizing defects but losing your customer base is like winning the battle but losing the war. The more time spent on the process itself can destroy the organization's capacity to capitalize on line-of-sight with the customer.

+ + +

SUPER HEROES OF BRIDGECULTURE
WHAT GREAT MANAGERS DO.

A supervisor in a highly respected, international research and polling firm sought out a select employee late Friday afternoon for a hurried moment of conversation:

"We need to talk…"

That was it—all that was said. Then the supervisor continued on her way, leaving demons in her wake. At such times, anxieties flourish, faults fly through the mind, jump-starting fears of failure, insolvency, and embarrassment. They faded in and out of the employee's subconscious throughout the weekend as she imagined one scenario after another in a sort of anxious "mental rehearsal."

> Touchpoints are moments where we connect with others - managers to their team members or people to their co-workers.
>
> Culture (good or bad) is built in these moments.
>
> +

Monday afternoon, the same manager, when (finally) reminded by our victim (a final humiliation added to the weekend of suffering), offered this dismissive response:
"Oh, I just wanted your chili recipe."

In that single touchpoint is the opportunity to build partnership, trust, and energy, or to drain those same things from the culture. In the hundreds of connections we have each day, are we connecting human passion to purpose—or using people up?

What do we need managers for? What do we need leaders for?

Much has been written about the importance of leadership and manager development and countless programs conducted, in person and via technology. We've spent money and trained people, spent money and trained people, but the results of these development activities have often fallen short of expectations.

We missed what was right in front of our eyes.

Every leader, manager, coworker, family member, and friend holds the power to help us see how we can build value in our role, as well as in the organization.

Until now, engagement research depicted people as pretty much at the mercy of their managers. Not entirely, but the prevalent view has been that managers are the key to the engagement and success of all their team members. It is the manager's job to set each person up to be successful.

That's a pretty tall order, isn't it? Particularly given that statistics suggest that only about 10 (maybe even 5) percent of managers are really effective enough to make this happen. Does that leave a full 90 percent of the managers off the hook?

Given the hours we work and the number of years we invest, that is an enormous proportion of our work/life satisfaction to hand over to someone we didn't personally select and may not invite to our summer barbeque. Even worse, it perpetuates the notion of people as victims of their environment, their organizations, and the people who manage them.

In every aspect of our lives outside of work, we function as adults; although to be fair, our effectiveness tends to vary with the venue. As consultants, we often see the disconnect between intentions and reality:

> One afternoon, we were returning to the rural production facilities of a Fortune 500 organization, accompanied by the plant manager. As we drove through the parking lot, he motioned to the array of pickups, SUVs, and other vehicles decked out with signs on the doors, hunting or fishing paraphernalia, and similar accessories of sport or commerce. Here's what he said:

> "Did you know that almost every employee in this plant has either another business part-time, coaches or teaches something, or is a master hunter or fisherman?

In every other aspect of their lives, our people are fully capable of managing their own businesses, raising families; they are leaders in the church, directors of local organizations—all on their own, completely self-starting and self-sufficient.

While at work, our single most common issue every week is trying to get them to take some responsibility for figuring things out on their own."[18]

Years later we are no closer to the solution to his dilemma. Whatever the popular theme this week, we are always trying to get our employees to _____(fill in the blank). You can read that as "innovate" or "take responsibility" or "make decisions like it's their business" or any number of other euphemisms for taking ownership.

The problem is not in the blank, the problem is in the stem of the statement: *"Trying to get them to..."*

The essential difference the plant manager was referring to was not the skill set, but the *inclination*. And the *locus of control* of that inclination makes all the difference.

Have you ever really worked at getting someone to do anything? In our experience, it seldom goes the way you imagined it. With kids, spouses, neighbors, or colleagues, people in general seem to take exception to being told what to do.

As human beings, we have a burning need to improve ourselves, exceeded only perhaps by the desire to improve others. Why is it that we can nearly always see a way *other people* can become more enlightened—become better employees, husbands, fathers, and salespeople?

Albeit well intentioned, our tendency to see "patently correctible flaws" in our colleagues, family members, and supervisors is a corollary of our farsightedness relative to our own shortcomings.
Consider how easy it is to see a solution when a person you know shares a personal problem. We can quickly sort the obvious factoids from the overtly emotional context and readily see X potential courses of action. Sometimes we fall victim to our own munificence and offer our patented solutions.

What does the person say in return?

Bless you! I never saw it with such clarity. I'll immediately stop mailing money to my sister and she'll leave her loser boyfriend and thank me for it for the rest of her life!

Not much chance. Generally, the recipients of our generosity respond with another verse of the same emotional constraints that bind them to their current course of action. These emotional constraints are usually explained in *pseudo-logic*,[3] but the underlying dimension is always feeling, not rationality.

> *If I stopped sending money to my sister, she would stop speaking to me, and that would make her even more dependent on her loser boyfriend.*

In contrast, our own problems are never that simple. That's because we actually feel the emotional constraints that bind us and, let's face it, ours are much more painful. When people reciprocate the favor and provide us with their rational and objective recommendations to our problems, we say, *"Thanks. But..."* as well. ("But" means disregard the previous sentence.)

This simple, all-too-human trait is the real reason that development begins with the individual and *not* in the mind of the manager.

The prevalence of learning and assessment systems has increased our tendency to develop people in accordance with *our definition* of what *they need*. Our survey instruments and our learning assessments give us evidence of both strength and weakness, so why not assign people to programs that systematically help them improve?

It has all the earmarks of a successful strategy. Too bad for us the situation is rarely that clear-cut or fixable. The automatic assignment of coursework presupposes that the person accepts our definition of the problem. As we noted above, that isn't always the case.

Moreover, it assumes that in addition to knowing *what* is wrong, we know *why*. This is a large assumption. We can see situations where the team is not engaged at work. We can even hypothesize that the problem may be related to the lack of relationship between the manager and the team. A week- or year-long intensive course in making friends and influencing people may increase that manager's repertoire of relationship-building skills. Yet in the final analysis, nothing is a substitute for the manager's authentic conversation *with* and concern *about* the team. The remedy lies in the manager's readiness/willingness to have that conversation, not the course of action proposed.

Similarly, the associate's role in his or her own self-improvement is all-important and cannot be shortcut by the intervention of a friend or manager.

---

[3] Pseudo-logic, like pseudo-outcomes, distracts us from the real thing. Recognizing the pseudo-variations keeps us focused on doing the right things in the right way.

Until we feel the need to change, other people's view of our need to change is essentially their problem and not ours.

This is certainly not to say that we don't need others to grow and develop; nothing could be further from the truth. We need another person—our manager, friend, or teacher—to hold up a mirror to us for insight and to encourage and partner with us as we stretch to reach new goals or achieve new abilities. But absent individual ownership, external reinforcement or prodding by others are ineffective substitutes.

At least twenty years ago, we wrote the phrase *You own your own development*. It is still true, and often underutilized as an organizational strategy. Why? Because we persist in wanting to "grow people" in our own way according to our definition of what they should be.

Perhaps it would be better to determine in what direction they are already moving and get out of the way?

+ + +

THAT WHICH SHALL NOT BE NAMED
HAS "MANAGER" OUTLIVED ITS USEFULNESS?

By now everyone knows that naming something provides energy or power to it, without which it may cease to exist:

> *He who shall not be named...*
> —Harry Potter and the Sorcerer's Stone[19]

> *Moment by moment the universe responds to our spoken and unspoken words and thoughts.*
> —The Secret[20]

One of the most implicit and recognized functions of the scientific process is to name a phenomenon and then progressively discover its properties and relationships. We have *Halley's Comet, pasteurization,* and *Parkinson's disease.* Social science

Does defining a mission in too narrow a term sentence an organization to obsolescence?

If Burlington Northern had conceptualized themselves as being in the "transportation business" as opposed to the "rail business", would there be a Burlington Northern Airline today?

+

is no exception, having coined such cultural giants as *anal-retentive*, *egocentric*, and the *Hawthorne effect*.

More specific to our own purposes, we evolved simply by understanding the distinction between merely *satisfying* employees and customers and *engaging* them (or increasing their loyalty).

The formerly empty space is first outlined—given a name—and then filled in and expanded upon with experiences...a concept is born.

The flip side of this process is that we become hamstrung when we refuse to extinguish outdated terms, attempting to attach new attributes to old nomenclature. Some terms should really be put out to pasture.

Consider the term *manager*. Perhaps it has outlived its usefulness and carries so much emotional baggage that it may no longer be eligible for reinvention?

For more than fifteen years, we have lived with *"It's the manager, stupid"* as a reality of the local work-unit culture. Yet, in spite of intensive development and focus, very little has seemed to increase the wholesale effectiveness of the management function.

Defining something can either limit or expand its possibilities.

Retiring the word manager might do more to improve the culture of an organization than any other one hundred things!

Why not call them *leaders*? We are not the first to suggest that a part of the problem lies in the term manager. The leadership wave hit nearly thirty years ago. At that time, organizations were retiring the word manager in favor of calling their managers leaders. Some still do. Their thinking was that it would result in a higher level of impact.

Yet the change desired from the linguistic shift never fully emerged, because the "leaders-in-name-only" were still bound by the expectations of their managerial role. The culture resisted the lure of the name because the emperor was still naked.[21]

> **What if we call them coaches?**
>
> One manufacturing organization elected to refer to the organization's supervisory personnel as "coaches".
>
> They reasoned that the connotative properties of "coach" are vastly superior to those of "manager" and were trusting in that power to deliver performance.

We can go from flying high in the zone to end up in a nonproductive lump on the floor of our offices based in large part upon our immediate supervisor.

No matter what we call them— manager, leader, coach—it is the range between the best and the rest that should demand our attention:

Great managers create bridges that connect their people to purpose; they empower, enable, enlighten, educate, and energize.

Poor managers control their people, disable the connections, depress, strain, and drain their energy!

+ + +

THE IN-OR-OUT LEADER, MANAGER, COACH
BEWARE THE TROLL BENEATH THE BRIDGE.

The concept of in-or-out leadership is quite easy to understand. In fact, Robert De Niro clarified it perfectly in *Meet the Parents.*

In the movie, De Niro points out to his prospective son-in-law, Ben Stiller that he would never truly be *in* the "circle of trust." Leaders are not always as verbal as De Niro, but their people get the message, nonetheless.

Think of the circle as the leader's domain where he or she controls time, reverence, and who gets heard. At any given time, there are people inside the circle and people outside the circle.

For those outside the circle, their world is driven by fear of never being allowed inside the circle.

Those inside the circle may be envied, but they are driven by fear of being put out of the coveted circle.

This may sound similar to the politics you experienced in middle school, because there are—unfortunately—many similarities between these two environments. All constituents are fearful, and thus their behaviors, choices, and decisions are all reflective of that fear.

Seemingly, the only real beneficiary of in-or-out leadership is the leader himself, as the leader is never challenged to see anything, including his or her own leadership, differently. Why? Because everyone (inside and outside of the circle) is fearful of creating any discord and consequently being either kept out or cast out.

Yet, for the leader, this results in an extremely myopic view of the world and reinforces a chronically inward-facing strategy. The only way this leadership influence can continue is for everyone to be constantly threatened regarding his or her position in the circle. When someone gets too comfortable being inside, he or she forces issues disrupting the equilibrium and thus needs to be kept in check.

The challenge to this model only occurs when certain players don't care if they are inside or outside the circle. The leader, with no leverage, has only one recourse: eliminate the person from the organization.

While this dynamic is so basic, it is precisely the reason why innovation, increased capacity, and growth are so difficult and complicated to achieve.

The nature of this model, "In and Out," demands conformity—everyone has to drink the metaphoric "Kool-Aid."

Innovation gets redefined as reasonable changes within a comfortable framework. Few big risks are taken, and work systems are kept in place regardless of their efficiency. Past innovations that defined the company are staunchly defended—carved in granite. Competitive advantage becomes a courtroom issue, and exciting, relevant innovations cease to exist. Great people flee these organizations and innovate elsewhere.

Leaders today are functioning under increased pressure to build value. The uncomfortable realization of "maybe it's me" is both frightening and liberating for the leader who has perpetuated this cycle.

Leaders must embrace those they need the most versus holding them hostage.

There is vulnerability in listening to the market, customers, and employees, being committed to hearing whatever they would say, rather than silencing them for comfort's sake.

This is one of the most difficult aspects of leadership—to self-assess. Nonetheless, to keep relevant, it behooves every leader and manager to ask: *Is it me?*

CAUGHT UP IN "IN OR OUT"

Many talented people have succumbed to the pressure of conforming to what their boss wants versus what the organization needs. Watching this scenario play out with a great leader we admire and respect, we witnessed first-hand the damage that it can do.

Paula, caught up in the hypocrisy of "in and out," battled her need to stay true to her personal values and still remain in the leadership circle. Time and again she was forced to act on decisions she did not agree with and found distasteful.

Straddling the line is a sort of cancer of the soul, and over time it eroded Paula's confidence, self-worth and health.

The continuing compromise and its consequences were like the famous T.S. Eliot poem: "ending not with a bang, but a whimper."

(T.S. Eliott, The Hollow Men, 1925)

THE CASE OF BUD

Bud, the CEO of a rapidly growing consumer products company, shared his story about a particularly difficult chapter in his career.

Bud was hired as the VP of sales for an employee benefits company. Like many organizations, there was a real disconnect between operations and sales. Recognizing the need to improve cooperation and communication between these two departments, Bud developed a plan to bridge the cleft.

Bud soon discovered that his counterpart in operations, Sarah, the VP of that department, wanted nothing to do with his "scheme." She believed the company's value was only in operations, not sales and marketing.

Despite operational resistance, Bud moved ahead with his plan, and it took hold. New sales were up, accounts were growing, and year over year, revenues increased. Service, processing, and customer-impact measurements all showed improvement.

It didn't take long before Sarah was threatened by the success of Bud's plan, even though the entire company had benefited.

A change in leadership occurred, resulting in Sarah becoming president.

One of the new president's first initiatives was a charge to grow revenues while simultaneously reducing sales bonuses by 30 percent. Bud couldn't disagree with the need for revenue growth, but he knew that his sales team would zero in on what they were losing. Concerned about the potential negatives, he wanted to bring something to the table for his team.

He created a special sales incentive program, called Kicker, for new account growth. While quarterly bonus payouts would still be cut, Kicker offered the potential to earn back the lost compensation.

Kicker was to be introduced at a national sales meeting. Bud asked Sarah, as the new president, to be there to support him and the sales team. She agreed.

Unfortunately, right before the compensation announcement, Sarah walked out of the meeting, indicating she had other more important priorities.

Bud went on to make the announcement to the sales team, focusing on what they could gain versus what they were losing. His team left the meeting feeling hopeful rather than discouraged, and the compensation system was an ultimate success.

The experience with the president, however, left Bud feeling powerless. He realized that his passion would always be secondary to the control needs of the new president. The writing was on the wall; with Bud's leadership compromised, it was time for him to leave.

In Bud's situation, the option to change the president was not up to him. What you can control in any situation is the action you will take, the attitude you have toward others, and the degree to which you persist. But you cannot control others or force them to change.

The president was comfortable within her circle. In turn, she cut herself off from the insight and perspective of Bud and the entire sales force.

Bud will tell you that this was a defining moment for him. He went on to new challenges and incredible success as a CEO of his own organization, but to this day, you can hear the despondency in his voice when he talks about this experience.

When, like Bud, you find yourself out of the circle and consistently unable to connect with purpose, the best course of action may be to depart.

+   +   +

MAKE A RULE, TAKE AWAY A CHOICE
THE CLOSER TO THE ACTION, THE BETTER THE DECISION.

In the world of horses, three times means a habit. Let your horse take a love nip and before you know it, you've got a horse that bites.

In the matter of ethics, it is what you do when nobody's watching that really counts. Consider this example:

We were in the company of representatives of a highly respected organization this spring, on a conference call where the parties were in three separate locations. The call had been arranged by Peter, a line manager within the organization, to introduce us to Sharon, the VP of HR, and her team.

Having participated earlier on the call, Sharon mistakenly believed her phone was muted and began to disparage Peter and his entire team. Still thinking she had muted the line, she belittled the people on the call and ridiculed their point of view.

Peter quickly intervened to inform her that her line was not muted and that her comments were being heard by the entire group. She quickly disconnected.

Peter apologized profusely to us and his own team for her lack of professionalism.

After more than thirty years in consulting, you would imagine we have heard it all, but Sharon's remarks were outrageous. Her comments about Peter, intended behind his back, were public both within and outside the company.

Quickly, we agreed that a cultural inquiry was required on our part, so we posed a few questions to the CEO.

Since your HR leader openly disrespected the process she is leading:

- *How do you think your people feel about leadership's commitment to your organization's values?*
- *Do you believe you can still inspire the trust of your people, or has that boat permanently sailed?*

The CEO did not respond. That made perfect sense to us, since this type of thing (hypocrisy) doesn't happen in organizations where integrity is nonnegotiable.

Doing the right thing has never been easy. Ask a soldier or anyone over sixty.

Or ask your children about the choices they are making at school every day. It is not a generational thing; it's a human thing. We frequently encounter a fork in the road where one of the paths appears to be downhill—easier, smoother, faster—and the other seems to be "the right thing."

A leader we greatly admire told us this story:

> *Just entering the shipping department late one afternoon, I interrupted a celebration with high-five hand-slapping and people laughing. The team members were so enthused, it looked like the group was about to hoist Joe onto their shoulders.*
>
> *This is exactly the kind of scene you want to run into all over your organization, and I was eager to get in the moment with them. I pressed for the news: What had happened? What was this success?*
>
> *With urging from the group, Joe told his story. It appeared that he had gone to Home Depot to pick up $1,800 of paint and the clerk forgot to charge him. That was the cause of the celebration.*

Our leader's response:

> *"Joe, get your ass back in the truck and go pay for the paint!"*

How naturally and spontaneously we can communicate our own values! Without a moment's hesitation, our leader sent an unequivocal message: *The misfortune of others does not count as our win; our success must be earned through work.* In the chaos and confusion of mistakes and misinterpretations, we find our way by always doing what is right.

There is no such thing as approximate integrity or an average amount of truth. Integrity starts at the top in a no-excuses/no-tolerance policy lived out by the CEO.

The disconnect between what we say and what we do is the stuff of movies, politics, psychoanalysis, and organizational culture. Research overwhelmingly supports the believability of nonverbal communication over verbal communication for just this reason.

Leadership must hold itself accountable to exceed the expectations it espouses for others. When a breakdown occurs, it opens a floodgate for everyone in the organization to justify his or her own behavior.

> *How can it be wrong for me to coach my brother-in-law on how to win a contract with my company when my congressman's face is permanently planted in the pork-belly trough?*

Most of us learned about bending rules in our first "training school"— aka our family. It begins with the definition of a little white lie and can potentially end with a series of betrayals that destroy trust and growth.

Great management and great leadership is all about knowing what must be held tightly (our values) and what must continually evolve (our methods); this is the "tight-loose" foundation for setting expectations with people.

What is a leader to do in the face of this paradox?

Determine your fundamental, unalterable rules. For those rules, make the lines between right and wrong absolute and tolerate no gray.

Don't make rules for the other stuff. Encourage the people closest to the action to use their line-of-sight and best judgment to make their decisions.

+ + +

MORE THAN "BUTTS IN SEATS"
CHOOSING THE RIGHT HORSE FOR THE COURSE.

"Only the best can play" is the theme song for premier organizations, from academic institutions and hospitals to sports teams, restaurants, and ice cream producers. We know a tiny little company that grew to a very large, prestigious one with that single thought.

Whatever the talent you collect, the culture will reflect.

If you covet aggressive, competitive, and striving people, you had better create an environment that honors speaking your mind and paying for performance and results. A culture of soft-spoken analytical people will need much more than passionate speeches to move them—the numbers, logic, and analysis had better be perfect.

For highly successful cultures, you need to put these two talent-related concepts into practice:

1) Tickets to admission.
2) Horses for courses.

Each different culture reveres certain talents, be it a knack for selling, consistency, or dependability. These can be thought of as "tickets to admission," because these tenets are so critical that people are not likely to flourish without them.

We know an amazingly successful organization—we'll call it AMMICIT—that is growing exponentially; its internal climate is highly competitive, combative at points, and hard-working beyond 99 percent of its peers. It is not uncommon to hear things that are both blunt and blue. The people who fit AMMICIT'S culture love the atmosphere, which is outrageous in its practical jokes, success, and extreme commitment, but the majority of professionals could never work there.

AMMICIT owns up to the fact; it isn't looking for "normal people" (because of its dominant growth goals and drive for talent). That is a good thing, because the average individual couldn't root and thrive in this extreme, high-performance culture.

Once the tickets to admission are punched, it's time to match the right horse to the right course.

In any horse-related contest, you must match your best thoroughbred, pony, or warm-blood to the course it will run. In terms of culture, a stable full of warm-bloods will give you power; a quarter horse will gain you breakout speed. Fill your company with just one type and you will be extremely vulnerable to a change in the playing field and expectations.

Some organizations deem certain roles too insignificant to be concerned about who inhabits them.

Our system is so well defined a monkey could do this job.
It doesn't matter who we hire—we just need butts in seats.

Hearing hiring managers describe jobs in terms like these makes it obvious the incumbents are seen as virtually interchangeable pawns on the chessboard. Often, analysis shows a different story.

Research with a large telemarketing firm revealed that some associates were so badly suited for their positions that the organization would be better off letting the customer service line ring, rather than allowing their worst players to answer and further alienate their customers.

Unlike horse racing, organizations don't always know the course they will need to run. Marketplace demands, new technology, and the speed of change itself mean the organization must be staffed to compete in whatever race is called.

People are much more than butts in seats and interchangeable pawns, they are the raw energy and talent for the organization's mission, vision, and purpose.

+ + +

FROM CONCEPT TO PLAYBOOK
WHEN LEARNING DOESN'T TRANSLATE INTO ACTION.

Leaders tend to "speak concept" but the team wants to hear specifics—they want to see the playbook.

One of the most challenging aspects of manager and leader development is the translation of concept into practice. The disconnect between what we try to teach and the results can range from disappointing to maddening.

Concepts and actions are the yin and yang within management and leadership development and both are necessary to generate results.

With decades of research in talent development behind us, we've seen that some truths are self-evident. First, learning does not always translate into being. Second, learning why the relationship between the manager and the associate is important doesn't always trigger the building of the relationship.

> My first teaching experience—an undergraduate class in communications—came with a stipend, but no instructor's manual. Less than a month into the position, I stumbled onto rock-solid evidence of cheating. In an envelope mailed directly to me, an uncle sent his niece's letter asking him to "fake an interview with her" along with his completed—and faked—feedback form. It was incontrovertible proof.

> I sought counsel with my faculty advisor, long-experienced in such things, and he responded with specifics: Bring her into your office, and hand her the letter. Say nothing.

> I executed it perfectly. I can still remember the scene: tears, anger, betrayal, confusion—and that was just my side of the encounter!

Becoming a better leader, manager, or teacher is personal and often painful. There are no guarantees and few shortcuts.

A long-time thought leader once insisted that we "train dogs" but "develop people," and this distinction has stayed with us for more than twenty years. In that one sentence, we gained insight into one of the most chronic challenges of the modern organization:

> We can effectively manage things, but we need to inspire, coach, and develop individuals.

The manager must emotionally understand the necessity of a trusting relationship before there is an authentic drive to improve or build one. That is why it always gets personal. Until someone can apply the concepts to his or her own life, that person cannot connect with the emotion necessary to internalize it.

In the course of in-depth interviews and research, people often tell us that becoming a parent was a life-changing experience. Prior to having kids, thinking about parenting is like learning about management without having anybody to manage. It feels sane, predictable, logical, and controllable—sounds rather nice, really.

It is only when you hear yourself reverting to your own parents' style (See: *If you don't stop crying, I'll give you something to cry about…Your face is going to freeze like that…If your friends jumped in the river would you jump in too?*) that you realize it is way more troubling to be a parent than it is to *imagine* being one. The imaginary parent has his or her own personal sitcom writer crafting the ending the parent prefers. The real parent knows that the episode never ends!

Managing people is a concept, but managing "Nicki" is a real-time, real-life challenge. Who knows how she'll respond?

The problem is that no amount of examples can ever protect us from real life, which throws one curveball after the other:

> I was coaching my daughter's second-grade Brownie troop when our city was threatened by a pervert using a puppy to lure young kids into his car. We invited a local policewoman to the troop meeting, and she led what we felt was a meaningful discussion with the girls. We queried them about what they would do if a stranger wanted them to look for a puppy or see his puppies, and they responded like savvy and committed machines.

> Just before refreshment, I tossed out one last question: What if someone was looking for his kitten?

The girls' response was equally sure: It was no problem helping a stranger with a kitten, just the stranger with the puppy.

The same thing can happen in organizations, where we concentrate on training rather than development. One of the most common ways to select employees is through their experience, particularly managers. It gives us a sense that the person has been there, done that. Unfortunately, a manager with ten years of experience may have just repeated his one-year managerial mistakes ten times!

That is precisely why development is a complex interaction of capability, concept, and experience.

The best cultures are obsessive about developing their bench:

Consider that in many organizations, managers, leaders, and supervisors account for approximately 10 percent of all their associates. Research tells us that mentors and coaches often learn as much and sometimes more than those they coach.

If each manager mentored or coached their top 20 percent of high performers, what could this combined 30 percent of the workforce accomplish?

✛ ✛ ✛

DEMOCRACY, BUREAUCRACY, ARISTOCRACY, MERITOCRACY
EVERYONE SHOULD BE CZAR (OF SOMETHING).

The MacroCulture of the United States stamps a democratic mentality on our youth from our first nonfamily cultural collision—kindergarten.[22]

- We are all equal.
- We all get to play.
- We all get to vote on things.
- No one is more important than anyone else.
- If we play nice, we get ice cream.
- We all line up and wait our turn.

It isn't until later in grade school and middle school that we come to understand the fine print associated with those same democratic principles.

- No two of us are equal in anything. Some things "count" much more than others, and on those things we are not equal.
- On some teams, everyone can play, but on the best teams, only the best players play.
- Very few really important things get decided by voting. Or, if they do, the voting took place before we came to the party (pun intended).
- Some people are lots more important than others.
- We don't always get what we deserve (that is both good and bad news).
- Some people are born at the front of the line, other people cut the line to get ahead, and a few never find the line.

The way we think things should be isn't necessarily the way things are.

As we become adults, we come to understand some of this in terms of merit, meaning the best players win. The democratic and meritocratic principles align in our thinking and coexist in relative peace.

In a bureaucracy, the owner of an idea is more important than the merit of that idea, and often the best ideas (or people) do not prevail. An individual's relationship with the power structure is often more significant than performance in predicting upward mobility. This is a little like aristocracy without the royal blood.

Most leaders prefer to think of their organizations as a meritocracy; they resist the notion that they've created and maintained a political power structure.

> *An entrepreneur we know, Ben, railed at the thought that his organization (a family-held aristocracy) was anything other than a "flat," performance-based organization where results counted more than connections. When Ben was adamant about the way something should be done but didn't want to mandate it, he would publicly bestow power to an associate by proclaiming them the "czar" of that particular function. Over the years Ben anointed czars of this and czars of that.*

The idea was that people would follow the czar. The culture, comprised of results-oriented professionals, was acclimated to the formal hierarchy but followed its own heroes, based on competency and performance.

The appointed czars rarely achieved any formal credibility. Productive people simply worked around the czar. In contrast, the informal leaders created and maintained a following that functioned effectively under the radar.

The lessons are universal: A culture will consistently sort out its leadership and its heroes based on its values.

You can confer a title and authority, but you can't assign credibility. That is earned.

To remain viable, an organization must be able to create and sustain growth. Its members are valued in relation to their ability to contribute to that mandate. That is why organizations must obsess over merit and performance above and beyond role, title, and function.

A people's choice leader who has earned the esteem of colleagues, associates, and customers through performance and service—that's the type of czar a culture needs to grow! An emergent leader has earned the right—through performance—to cast a heavier shadow.

Why, given our almost desperate need for innovation, performance, and growth, is the emergence of true leaders such a cultural long shot?

+ + +

LOSE THE LABELS
GAIN THE CONNECTION.

At nearly every assembly for human performance improvement, you can hear the participants leaving the sessions, processing their new self-definition in the latest language:

> *"I'm a Sagittarius, future-thinking, Woo Cat, but I've got a certain conscious competence in perception in spite of my introversion."*

It makes us want to institute a no-jargon zone.

What self-awareness we may have gained through assessments is almost always truncated by the labels we learn to apply to ourselves. Our focus quickly shifts from what we feel to what "achievers" feel or what "dominant drivers" like to do.

Labels can be limiting and potentially hurtful.

We've learned it over and over again from the various diversity studies and sensitivity seminars we've been a part of. As a result, our assessment protocols insist there are no good talents or bad talents—just differences.

Do you think that people actually believe that?

Have you considered that labels are also harmful to the process of connecting? They don't encourage unique expression.

As consultants who have deliberately worked to create a language for communicating, it seems our efforts have been a bit *misdirected*. Once we created the schema, we became more concerned about teaching people the right terms to use rather than being interested in what the people really *needed* to say—we became labelers.

> *Our cell phones offer us more than two hundred applications that can bring us cost comparisons on anything we want to buy. We can scan our surroundings to grab coupons that apply at that moment and point to stores that offer the products we need.*

> *We can start our smart ovens from our phones and turn on our dryer, lights, and DVR from anywhere in the world. We could adjust our underground sprinklers, but the weather link from the satellite has already done it for us.*

At a time when we are all embracing the virtually limitless potential and complexity of our technology, organizations are trying to shut down human variability. We see people increasingly attracted to explanations of human behavior that label us in terms of our strengths, competencies, drives, and engagement levels—and to what end?

We've been known to say: People are messy creatures and quite frequently defy categorization. But more accurately: Labeling people is limiting, destructive, and essentially impossible!

What matters is that people feel understood, and that is a long, long way from a label.

+ + +

SEND YOUR MANAGER HOME DAY
. . . AND SEE IF YOU MISS HIM.

Take Your Daughter to Work Day was a way of helping young women expand their notions of themselves and showing them that they are capable of determining their own future and not subject to the limitations of societal expectations. To some extent, the Take Your Daughter to Work Day has worked.

In fact, it may have worked so well that one mother told us:

> *When my daughter left for college, I think she was trying to send me a not-so-subliminal message:*

> *Things I don't need my mother for: Reminding me to be careful (again), worrying about my study habits, and asking if I get enough sleep...*

Perhaps it is time to organize a Send Your Manager Home Day in its place? We could institute the following rules:

> *Before your manager leaves, you need to list (in writing) all the things you don't need her for.*

> *You know the list: checking up on you, stating the obvious, reminding you of the things you never forget, giving lip service to your contributions...*

Reading this type of list can feel brutal at first, and when we face such things (from our associates or from our family) we tend to react somewhat defensively—*who, me?!* But on second sight, the list can be enlightening and liberating.

It is likely that the list a daughter or son would make regarding what she *does* need her parents for would be telling in its brevity yet meaningful in the extreme:

> *Trust me, support me, give me time to prove myself, and—wait for me to come to you!*

We think the same would be true for most of our team members. We need our managers, but not to be our conscience or our parent.

After Send Your Manager Home Day, we would want to welcome our managers back with a reminder.

Dear Manager,

Here's what we really need you for:

You are the tender of our MicroCulture. If you don't help us to find our best fit, we may suffer the indignity and disappointment of struggling at tasks for which we are not well suited.

You see first-hand the energy on our team. Help us to feel a stronger sense of purpose from our work—talk to us about our line-of-sight with our partners and customers.

You are the only one who can run interference for us with the structure, the policies, and process that sometimes limit us. Help us remove the barriers.

Trust in us to make decisions, and stand by us when we do. We are close to the action, and we are committed to doing the right thing for the customer.

Please connect us. Help us close the gaps and bridge the silos that separate our team from our extended family—the other departments and teams with whom we partner to deliver our products/service.

You are the eyes and ears of leadership—their link to us. Help them know what we need to be successful and that we are ready to be full partners in achieving our mutual goals.

Sincerely,
Your Team

FINDING WALDO AT WORK
PURPOSE BUILDS THE BRIDGE

Purpose is the hallmark of BridgeCulture—the guiding principle that inspires innovation, service, and partnership. A high-performance culture has a true servant focus that is derived from its mission and purpose; it puts a high premium on service to the customer and sees that those values are acted on, inside and outside the organization.

When actions are disconnected from values, the culture squanders the precious energy of its people in a way that adversely affects the customer's experience and chips away at the brand promise. Efficiencies that sacrifice value are ill-guided short-term solutions that can end up costing more than they save.

The essence of successful BridgeCulture is tied to the unique value proposition of the organization, such as the customer's viewpoint.

SQUEEZING THE MIDDLE ≠ GROWTH

The perception of value is at the heart of nearly every decision we make, from family decisions and grocery store decisions to business decisions and political decisions. *How much value am I getting here?*

> *Consider providing orthodontic treatment for your children. It begins like anything else: in a waiting room, waiting. Then it proceeds into a flurry of appointments lasting only fifteen minutes; this goes on for the better part of a decade. The children are crying; your savings are whittling away like an oak twig beneath the blade of a bearded woodworker. The children complain and stare at you with watery eyes... please make it stop. No, you tell them. This is important, it's worth it. All the other parents are doing it.*

> *But at what point do you crack? At what point do you throw in the towel, move away, and raise your children among the crooked-toothed masses? Is it really worth it? All of that money, all of that time? I guess nobody will know until high school graduation, when that perfect smile shines across the gymnasium. Is that smile worth it?*

The conventional approach suggests that as we make things less costly (lower the price), the customer enjoys an even greater value. Thus, we offer sales and savings to urge customers to buy more. Who doesn't see the wisdom in that?

In Anytown, USA, our local furniture stores hold sales for Presidents' Day, Father's Day, Independence Day, Boss is Gone Day, and our personal favorite, the No-Sale Sale Day. In fact, furniture stores actually need to have a new sale every week, because people won't visit when they don't!

The furniture-business sale strategy has inadvertently lowered value in the mind of its customers. Instead of seeing the sale price as a bargain, customers see the normal price as out of proportion to the value.

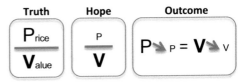

Any time the price and value are out of proportion to one another, there's dissonance. And the perception of value must be reconciled with price in the customer's mind.

One of the world's largest consumer products companies, facing competition from inexpensive brands, elected to lower the price of their own flagship product. They believed this would help them to compete.

Consumers quickly exposed the flaw in the organization's strategy. The branded product wasn't viewed as a real "steal" in the market; instead it lost its appeal and value. The customer's perception of quality decreased commensurate with the lowered price.

Whenever price drops, so does the value in the customer's mind. What happens when price increases?

While working with a large industrial manufacturing firm, we had the opportunity to research the way customers perceive value when prices are constantly fluctuating. Much of the perception of value depended upon the way customers experienced the change through their sales representative, the way they *heard* it. A closer look revealed that the representative's own perception played an important role in how the customer reacted to the change:

Facing the price increase, one salesman, Richard, would say, "I'm as mad about this as you are. I can't believe they did this. I'm just the messenger; I didn't have anything to do with the decision."

In contrast, their best salesperson, Denise, took a decidedly different approach with her clients. Having communicated the change, she then accompanied the first delivery to every one of her customers, to make sure it was a successful transition and the customer was happy with the entire process.

The manner in which Denise presented the change created an opportunity for a stronger partnership with the customer, moving them through the process and establishing greater value. Richard's approach, throwing the company under the bus, further disconnected the customer.

What about when the value is high and the price is low? Try selling a Mercedes SL550 Roadster for $15,000. What is the first thing a potential customer might say?

"What's wrong with it?"

We've seen mega players operate this way, opting to gain market share at almost any cost, lowering prices into the pits of despair: *We've got to buy their business.*

"No, don't do it!" we say. But once they get that crazy idea in their head, there's no stopping them. When the price drops, so does the value-perception. Once done, it is difficult to ever increase that value in the mind of the customer. So long, farewell, auf Wiedersehen, good-bye.

Buying and selling homes teaches many lessons in value. In a real estate transaction, sellers are often outraged at having to pay 6 percent of their home's sale price to a Realtor.[23]

 Of those homeowners, about 10–15 percent will opt to save the commission and sell the home themselves.

Buyers looking for bargains are also increasingly savvy. They know that homes represented by real estate professionals include commissions, and so they often look at For Sale by Owner[24] homes to save the commission.

Can both the buyer and the seller "save" the same 6 percent?

Let's consider a home where the market value is $500,000. Market value is based on the actual sold price of commensurate homes, regardless of representation.

With representation:

> *The buyer pays $500,000.*

> *The seller's net is $470,000, or the sold price minus the 6 percent commission for the Realtor. In this case, the buyer always pays the commission or finances it as a part of the sale price.*

Without representation:

> *For the buyer to save the 6 percent, the seller must agree to sell the home for $470,000 (which would be the same net price if the seller had used the services of a real estate professional).*

For the seller to save the 6 percent, the buyer must pay $500,000 with no representation.

Either the buyer or the seller can win, but not both on the same transaction. We say: If the buyer is saving, the owner is paying, and vice-versa.

In reality, the actual market value of For Sale by Owner homes is significantly lower than the average commissions charged by real estate firms. This means that the buyer usually wins, and these buyers are usually savvy real estate investors (not novice or occasional home buyers). The seller rarely gains anything in the For Sale by Owner game, so, to quote the professionals, "Why not use a Realtor and have it done right?"

Interestingly, when neighborhoods are predominately non-represented (all For Sale by Owner properties), the sold prices cause a decrease in market value for the neighborhood in comparison to surrounding neighborhoods that remain fully represented. This results in a net loss of value.

Organizations have worked to improve perceived value by focusing on technology and quality. With processes like Lean and Six Sigma, companies have "saved" billions of dollars in time and efficiencies, with commensurate increases in quality. Businesses have lowered the cost of production with offshore manufacturing and improvements in technology.

Where did that money go? Can both the organization and the customer save the same amount?

This leadership theme has resulted in the "Walmarting"[25] of our organizations.

Cost-based pricing means that the organization lowered the price by making gains in production. *We offered our products to our customers at reduced costs, which they passed along to their customers.*

And our overall result has been a huge reduction in value!

Ten years ago, the price of a fifty-inch flat-screen plasma television was approximately $9,000.

Technology has improved the product and reduced the cost to $2,500 at any local big box retailer.

The decreased price means that value has dropped out of the plasma television market.

The only hope left then is volume. This reminds us of a classic sales story:

> *Two brothers go into business together buying raw fleece, carding it, finishing it, and then selling the cloth at the market. In painstaking detail, they explain their time-consuming and rigorous methods to their father.*
>
> *His reaction: "So, you did all this work and actually lost $2 in the process?"*
>
> *The brothers exchange glances and nod smugly. "Yep...but we plan to make it up with volume."*

Why do people shop at Walmart? *To save money.* Walmart has perfectly sculpted their market to reflect their strategy. Their only differentiation is their price. When customers shop at Walmart, they make a clear choice.

What must happen internally to sustain a strategy that strips out value? The organization:

- Is forced to continuously sell more, because the margins are tight.
- Must constantly chisel suppliers and force them to produce more at lower prices.
- Needs to keep squeezing the middle to sustain earnings.

"The middle" refers to everything between the raw goods we purchase and the products or services we deliver to our customer. This constant *squeezing* causes the profit margins to continuously decrease; they may even slide to zero just to stay in business. Like the two brothers, the only hope is making it up on volume.

Do we have to produce things more cheaply because of economic demands? Consider this: As a nation, we were in cost-cutting mode long before the economy tanked:

- In the 1960s and '70s, clothing manufacturers put jobs in China for fifty cents an hour and thought it was the miracle that would save them.
- During the tech boom, companies found programmers in India and cut a massive amount of costs.

Both of these industries, however, have since leveled out. Costs always catch up to you.

When you build a company on cost savings, you become a slave to the middle part of your value statement. And the middle is where culture lives.

+ + +

TRUSTING LINE-OF-SIGHT
PROCESS, POLICY, AND ACTION ALIGNED TO THE RIGHT OUTCOMES.

Every person in the organization is ultimately charged with a shared critical outcome: to attract new customers and retain current ones. Line-of-sight to the customer creates motivation, positive energy, and collaboration.

The challenge with this is that many jobs are far from customer sales and direct contact with current customers, so employees with fuzzy line-of-sight miss out.

When people are struggling at work, sometimes the key lies in reminding them about what their purpose is—how what they do contributes to the acquisition and retention of customers.

Let's face it, quality is about the value of what we hand off. If we're not able to see the broader purpose, we may become complacent, simply checking off boxes with no concern for the ultimate outcome.

Our data suggests that there are rarely more than four links in the chain to line-of-sight. Many times it is only two. If the flow of energy isn't well choreographed, internal conflict erupts, silos form, and the true victim is the customer.

Uninterrupted energy is positive energy and sets forth a cycle of purpose, satisfaction, and renewal for every role (job) in the organization. This paves the way for added value, focusing on the right things at the right time.

Leaders want growth and value.

Managers want increased productivity.

Employees want to contribute.

The new reality of how we connect emotionally to our work is not all that complicated. The "wants" at each level do not conflict or compete with one another; in fact, they are highly complementary. But often our policies and procedures are not.

Research in a highly productive call center revealed that procedures designed to increase sales were too often scaring off both customers and representatives.

> Customer service reps were required to up-sell four times before accepting the customer's decision not to buy. From a statistical perspective, this process resulted in additional sales. What was not apparent at face value was the resulting impact on the actual customer service representative and on customer loyalty.

> One top-performing rep, Melissa, recounted an incident with a customer who had called to request some account changes due to the death of her husband. Facing the distress and tears of the widow, the rep was forced to continue up-selling or risk receiving a reprimand. Melissa told us, "This job really isn't worth it."

> Representatives torn between service to the customer and personal success (i.e., commission structure) became disillusioned with the organization, updated their resumes, and sought other venues for employment—au revoir!

When the policies of our organizations conflict with the principles they profess to live by, employees lose confidence in themselves, the stated values, and the organization. As a result, the entire team operates on depleted energy.

Most policies are all about the what but not the why.

In contrast, high-performance cultures keep the line-of-sight to the customer alive. One leader regularly asked employees to map out their relationship to the customer:

> "Those were ah-ha moments for people...They had forgotten that their reason for being was about the customer, particularly if they worked at corporate. The accounting folks needed to know how their job creates great service for the customer."

When every person in the organization has line-of-sight to the customer, the energy is focused for growth.

BRINGING STILLS TO LIFE

Perhaps it would be best to write policies as folklore that emphasizes the "why" behind the "what," and brings the principle to life.

J. Peterman does this in their catalogs (which are referred to as "Owners Manuals." They sell clothes using drawings (rather than pictures) then attach an "attitude" via a story.

"FOLLOW ME"

Some of us are followers. Some of us are leaders.
Facts are facts. This hat is for leaders.
However, should a follower pick up this hat, they will be looked on as a leader and discover hidden leadership skills.
"Reservations won't be a problem."

The J. Peterman Panama (No. 1015). Highest grade toquilla fibers; woven, as are the best panamas, in Ecuador. The "technology" which made summers in the Canal Zone bearable. Almost. Rakish black grosgrain band. Devastating brim. Slightly intimidating. Women will whip it off your head and insist on trying it on. Men may put a fist through their inferior versions.

www.jpeterman.com/Dad-Stuff/The-J-Peterman-Panama

✦ ✦ ✦

There are other important and highly interrelated aspects of culture, but the test of the culture actually lies in its ability to create organic growth by connecting and developing its people's line-of-sight to the customer.

+ + +

SUMMARY: BRIDGING OUTCOMES
CORNERSTONES OF PERFORMANCE.

Recurring themes cross over from the MicroCulture into the BridgeCulture, things like belonging, relationship, purpose, line-of-sight, structure, and individuality. These consistencies emerge as cultural cornerstones influencing the organization's energy and performance.

In the MicroCulture, the foundation of the organization's energy, we recognize the impact of a strong fellowship with team members, a thoughtful relationship with managers, and a strong line-of-sight to the purpose; we see beyond the job description to the importance of each individual's fit for his or her role. These elements depend on the effectiveness of the team, which means the health and vitality of MicroCultures lie beyond leadership's immediate control.

Within the BridgeCulture, these same themes present themselves again in different forms. Relationships are critical to connect various teams to one another and to keep the organization's focus on line-of-sight. Individuality and structure struggle against each other within the confines of policies and procedures. The most successful managers translate these barriers to create maximum energy, while the least successful allow process to take precedence over their people.

Exemplary levels of performance are achieved only when the culture is aligned with the brand and customer expectations. This requires a relentless interest in the moment-to-moment interactions that build energy and deliver the organization's unique brand promise.

These moments culminate into the broader organizational culture, the MacroCulture. Importantly, however, MacroCulture is not a separate culture, but rather a reflection of these powerful Micro- and BridgeCultures within.

MacroCulture isn't what leadership expects it to be. It is what it is.

Section Four
MACROCULTURE: MORE INTERESTED THAN INTERESTING
THE MUSIC OF HIGH PERFORMANCE CULTURES.

Many parents have wandered down the piano-lesson path with mixed results. Plenty of people know how to play "Chopsticks," but only a minuscule few follow through and actually master the instrument.

Like parents, organizations have a tendency to buy the piano when what they really want is to hear the music.

From a simple melody to a complex concerto, companies yearn to hear something that does not exist solely in the piano, but only when the instrument is connected with a human player.

Throughout our interviews, organizations have regaled us with stories about their MacroCulture, but what they were describing was the piano, not the music. These aspects—structure, departments, job descriptions, and workflow—comprise the visible frame of the piano. These tangible elements are all a part of the rational organization.

In fact, your organizational piano probably looks a lot like everyone else's, even though the music you intend to play (your brand promise) is completely unique.

Leaders focus on the strategy, the vision, the mission—the "score" they intend to play, but what they are so anxious to create is as elusive as music itself, which can never be played *exactly* the same way twice.

This, too, is the defining element of culture. It cannot be stored; it lives and evolves (or devolves) moment by moment.

> Some estimate that there are 240,000,000 pianos throughout the world. We wonder how many of those pianos are played frequently, only occasionally, and how many are not played at all?
>
> ✦

The "culture plaque" on the wall at Transemco proclaims the organization's values: dignity and respect, performance, customer service, teamwork, and integrity.

We love these values and look forward to seeing them in action.

Walking onto the third floor of the Transemco building, no one greets us or makes eye contact. They don't acknowledge us, or even each other.

Up on the fifth floor, we hardly move a foot before we are welcomed. People introduce themselves and, in turn, their colleagues. Everyone is curious; they ask us who we are, what we are looking for, and how they can help.

Which floor embodies the MacroCulture of Transemco?

They both do.

There isn't one singular MacroCulture that describes an organization; the MacroCulture is interpreted by the people within it. The people make the music.

In fact, the only way to understand a culture is through the hearts and minds of its people. More specifically, how the employees experience the culture. High-performance cultures require leaders who are more *interested in* their people's perspectives than their own. Yes, the leaders' ability to extend a vision is important, but not at the expense of understanding how their people are translating this vision into action.

> As hard as they may try, leaders can't mandate culture.
>
> But they can accentuate its best qualities.
>
> +

Leaders must take an interest in how the organization's traditions are interpreted and translated by its members and the relationship between the culture's science and its religion (i.e., the things that can and should change versus those that can't and shouldn't). The ramifications of how outcomes are measured and celebrated—and heroes created—should garner the interest of leaders.

Throughout this section, we'll focus on leadership's role in cultivating culture. Taking an active interest in it as it bubbles up from the local MicroCultures and managerial levels (BridgeCultures) within the organization. At every point, from the MicroCulture to the BridgeCulture and culminating in the MacroCulture, leadership's role is to insure that every level aligns with the strategy and brand promise to create competitive advantage.

+ + +

TRADITIONS, TRADITIONS
WITHOUT THEM, OUR LIVES WOULD BE AS SHAKY AS A FIDDLER ON THE ROOF!

In the unforgettable story *Fiddler on the Roof*, the hero and father, Tevye, attempts to hold tight to the traditions of his culture, which are being threatened by his daughters, society, economics, and the political pressures of the time.

Traditions are a comfort to us; they provide the answers to questions we no longer need to ask.

They paint our roles and tell us how to act, how to dress, and what to revere. Our traditions create expectations for shared experiences. Some are written, and others are kept in mind by the traditionalists within the culture itself.

Representing the history, rituals, and mores of the culture, we rarely concern ourselves with the "why" behind our traditions. *Fiddler on the Roof* could be the story of any father, in any generation, who commiserates about the last great generation to the next generation.

Our traditions exemplify much more than the rational events of the past—they represent the emotional essence of it.

The foundations of our culture are not merely stuff from history, but actually contribute to the development of our individual and collective character. Like Tevye, who ultimately comes to appreciate the core of his life's values distinct from those traditions, we need to separate the wheat from the chaff.

The traditions of the modern organization continually color and shape our thoughts. What will we do to get the keys to the corner office and executive washroom?

In the intelligent satire *The Ape in the Corner Office: Understanding the Workplace Beast in All of Us,* Richard Conniff presents a number of examples of corporate rituals that appear to have their roots in our very extended family—chimpanzees, orangutans, and the like:

> In the modern workplace, the business of dominance and submission
> is usually most effective when it is least obvious. Almost all of the
> aggression gets channeled into symbolic forms. That's the main
> function of job titles, big offices, power clothes (as the phrase "Armani
> armor" suggests), the seating order at meetings, important friendships,
> ample expense accounts, and other signs of power or status...
>
> This is the first lesson about social dominance: It rarely involves overt
> physical force.[26]

The trappings of power are among the traditions of organizational culture.
Size matters in the desks, chairs, window coverings, and office space, for
these items signify our progression to pack leadership. This is especially
true in the new flatter structures. It isn't always about performance or
other such things, but about symbolic objects.

Implicit within most organizational cultures are the rewards of membership
associated with tenure. Tenure, or time in grade or LOS (length of service),
is a cultural tradition that carries enormous implications. Talk about moving
the cheese! What happens when you work for twenty years for the keys to
the office with a view and find they've replaced it with a desk in the center
of the room?

> In corporate Japan, people are more or less provided a job for life.
> While it is changing, there still remains an obligation by corporations to
> keep people employed at just about all costs. This is especially true for
> those grandfathered in before the mid-1990s.
>
> While corporations feel obligated to keep people employed, they also
> have tricks to get these employees to quit—"the window job (mado
> giwa zoku)." Instead of firing someone, corporations will sometimes
> give him or her a mado giwa zoku with absolutely nothing to do. People
> in these positions come to work and gaze out the window, thinking of
> what life would have been like if...

Research indicates that tenure is one of the most confusing cultural
variables for high-performance cultures.

**Tenure: as a badge of loyalty and persistence, we revere it; as a
gatekeeper to progress, we fight it.**

Consider this example where tenure is irrelevant:

> *In American football, if the rookie performs, the rookie gets the job. If the ten-year veteran performs, he gets the job.*
>
> *What if we staffed our football line-up by tenure?*

No wonder we are confused when organizations systematically replace their long-term, highly paid employees with cheap, inexperienced people. Take Circuit City for instance, whose infamous problems were exacerbated when they fired their most experienced salespeople, which pundits say sped up the financial problems that led to their bankruptcy:

> *In 2007, Circuit City laid off its 3,400 highest-paid salespeople because management bean counters thought they were costing the company too much.*
>
> *The layoffs were especially crippling because the highest-paid salespeople were the best and most experienced salespeople. Without its top sales staff, sales slowed to a crawl and the quality of Circuit City's customer service tanked.*[27]

Traditions will inevitably be broken or changed by newcomers. Each generation challenges the status quo as each new hire arrives with fresh ideas about how the organization *should* work. Both sides—the traditionalists and the newcomers—have a dog in the fight. The newcomers question things that don't make sense, while the traditionalists defend the house of cards that took so much time to build.

The culture reacts to the tradition-breaking in predictable ways, by holding onto the what and trying to find a rational way to explain the why.

A wise newcomer should attempt to understand, before challenging the status quo, and a wise culture should entertain those challenges in a way that keeps the spirit of innovation alive. But in many cases, the tug-of-war results in a net loss.

Organizational cultures protect their traditions by maintaining a façade of rationality. Does it really take each employee *eight years* to progress from Accountant I to Accountant II, from Accountant II to Supervisor of Accounting? Does this tradition have any practical significance?

It seems reminiscent of a similar tradition popular in grade school: *line up and wait your turn.*

Companies find structural ways to make people wait their turn. They say, "But it's a rule!"

Union cultures are famous for their traditions, which have been written into laws. This is an extreme example of codifying *appropriate* behavior to make it impervious to challenge by upstarts or efficiency experts. It no longer has to stand the test of making sense (or cents) to future generations of new hires; it must be negotiated, as if the value were inherent.

The thicker the policy manual, the less effective the organization becomes and the greater the cost to enforce the rules. Oftentimes, unions are an impediment to change for precisely this reason. Like the superego, the position of the union is often at odds with the organization's survival goal.

HE SAID-SHE SAID: UNION TROUBLES VS EXECUTIVE GREED

The recent Hostess bankruptcy is a classic case of finger pointing, with some blaming the bakers' union refusal to ratify a new contract strike (a 92 percent vote) and their subsequent strike for the company's implosion. They point to union rules that propagated union jobs by limiting productivity:

1) no truck could carry both bread and snacks even if going to the same location;

2) drivers could not load their own trucks; and

3) the same workers could not load both bread and snacks.

For their part, union members defend their moves, pointing to the $110 million dollars in concessions back to the company in return for promised new technology, which never materialized after the 2004 bankruptcy. Union officials attributed the collapse to a string of leadership debacles including six CEOs since 2002 and the consistently high salaries paid to executives throughout these difficult times. Still the judge awarded $1.8 million in bonuses (in addition to their usual compensation) for 19 Hostess executives during the approximately yearlong company wind-down and sale.

Of late, the accusations seem pretty well-substantiated on both sides. The loss? Approximately 18,500 jobs.

✦ ✦ ✦

SCIENCE AND RELIGION
WE NEED INNOVATION TO REVITALIZE AND LIVE OUT OUR RAISON D'ÊTRE.

Thinking of culture from the perspective of both science and religion offers us a new, highly instrumental lens through which to understand it.[27]

Culture as religion reflects the underlying values that remain constant and forever true. It is not the products themselves, but the *customer's needs* that reflect the core of our religion. These needs give us our purpose and our mission.

Science reflects the methods we use to achieve our goals. Like strategies, our science must continually evolve to keep us on the cutting edge. Organizations are in a constant change-effort to make things better, faster, and more relevant to the marketplace.

Consider Michelin, an organization which embodies both science and religion.

> *Their long-standing religion is "to enhance the mobility of people and goods." This conviction, their North Star, has guided critical decisions and been instrumental for their product development, growth, and success.*

> *Their religion has guided the science, which is always evolving and creating relevance and applications.*

> *An example of science evolving from religion started with a rubber brake pad, called "The Silent" in 1889. Then in 1892, the Michelin brothers scattered nails along a bike race as a way of introducing their first, "removable" bike tire, preventing a flat tire from ending a journey. The Michelin Red Guide published in 1900, provided the traveler with an instruction guide and reference book to enhance the travel experience. In 1984, the company developed the first radial tire for motorcycles. On July 21, 2011, the final space shuttle flight landed on Michelin tires. The science continues.*

> *At Michelin, they call their commitment: "ceaseless innovation."[28]*

Some organizations hold on too long to a narrow definition of who and what they are; others chase profit windmills over their real mission and purpose. The best-in-class harness science to their religion and evolve in a way that promotes excellence and long-term service to their customers.

Organizations continuously need new science to help revitalize and live out their true purpose, their religion.

Cultures must hold tight to their religion in the face of rampantly changing technology, methods, structures, and processes. The challenge is to know what must change and what should be preserved.

What role does religion play?

Religion is the bedrock, the foundation, the values—it's the essence. While values are necessary, we've found that 90 percent of the mission and value statements painted on corporate walls are essentially the same. There's very little power within these values to inspire the people—to stir something within. Values can't do it alone; they are insufficient to create the kind of passion vital to strong cultures.

Do you know the religion of your culture? We posed this question to a client recently. His response:

> *"We have no religion. We just have Hindus, Buddhists, Methodists, and Presbyterians around here. Everyone came from a different company in our industry and brought their old religion with them! Now ours is just a collection, not a common, true religion."*

> **Is Culture More Science or Religion?**
>
> If culture were a scientific phenomenon, it would have to play by the same rules and follow predictable laws. We could reliably control and manufacture the improvements we desired.
>
> If culture were a religious phenomenon – we would have to accept that it is out of our hands.
>
> In reality, it reflects both.

What's important about religion is that it has the capacity to stir our emotions. People get passionate about their religion. If there's passion, organic movement will follow.

> *For the Mayo Clinic, health isn't a value, it's the real deal—health is religion. It is part and parcel of everything that defines the Mayo Clinic and creates a bond of loyalty beyond that of other institutions and practices.*

Religion helps a culture transcend itself.
It encourages the culture to expand in the pursuit of the organization's true purpose. Religion doesn't describe market, strategy, or product as much as it defines the *why* of an organization.

It doesn't need to be complicated. It can be as simple and enduring as the Hippocratic mantra: "First, do no harm." (We seriously doubt the AMA will ever come out and change it to "OK, a little harm is fine.") Our religion defines our shared belief, guides our choices, and leads our way to the future. It doesn't limit—it directs with purpose.

Don't hire an ad agency to write it for you. It doesn't need to be meticulously wordsmithed or carefully crafted. Rendering your religion onto a silver plaque and hanging it beside your mission statement won't help.

Religion is unique because its primary role is only fulfilled when we passionately express that religion in our own distinctive way and in the service of others.

Much like a sermon, which may include complicated nuances and interpretations of scripture, your religion's real function is to inspire members of the congregation. No matter that they don't understand the intricacies, it only matters that they live out their faith.

In the movie *Pay it Forward*, Haley Joel Osment, starring as young Trevor, responds to the challenge of his teacher, played by Kevin Spacey:

> *Trevor's assignment was to think of something to change the world and then put it into action. He comes up with the idea of paying the favor forward, rather than paying it back. By repaying good deeds with new good deeds done to three new people, Trevor's moves start a revolution, not just for him and his mother, but also for his teacher and an ever-expanding group of strangers.*

AMAZON: Amazon's vision is to be Earth's most customer centric company; to build a place where people can come to find and discover anything they might want to buy online.

STARBUCKS: Our mission: to inspire and nurture the human spirit – one person, one cup and one neighborhood at a time.

FACEBOOK: Facebook's mission is to give people the power to share and make the world more open and connected.

This movie, released in 2000, stimulated the Pay It Forward Movement, whose slogan is "Changing the world one favor at a time" and which has recorded spontaneous acts of kindness all over the world. This is another example that a simple religion can rouse the passion and action of the people.

Religion cannot exist without people. From the preservation of the planet for future generations to the development of self-worth in children, religion is the stuff of human inspiration, passion, and service.

> *Recently, a CEO was lamenting the difficulty in communicating his vision to the organization. His VP of HR reminded him that it takes repetition and offered the following guidance:*

> *(1) Tell them what you are going to tell them; (2) tell them; and (3) remind them again what you told them.*

Our counsel differed. Leadership's thinking can become so pervasively and subliminally top- down, that they may not always recognize how this orientation distorts their approach or actions.

You may be tempted to think of your religion as the *grand vision* of what can be accomplished and that it is this grand vision that inspires your people to selfless action and the pursuit of excellence—very noble, indeed.

The opposite may be the case.

Inspiration comes in all forms, from the smallest of details to the grandest of visions.

Perhaps the most inspiring element of your religion comes from the smallest act of kindness or compassion when it's least expected— preserving the dignity of an elderly patient or celebrating the excitement of a young husband's first do-it-yourself plumbing project. The service provider (nurse's aide or sales associate) can experience passion in the simple connections that give meaning to their role and accumulate value for the organization.

Science tends to intrude on these experiences by dictating the methods and measuring the elements rather than the meaning. Science is about efficiency; religion is about emotion.

The test of religion lies in this question: To whom does it matter?

- If it only matters to the organization (profit, efficiencies, market share, and volume), it reflects our science.
- If it matters to the customer, the client, the families, the patient, and the community, it reflects our religion.

+ + +

IF IT IS NOT IMPROVING, IT IS DETERIORATING
SCIENCE IS CONTINUOUS IMPROVEMENT AND DISRUPTIVE INNOVATION.

It isn't unusual for organizations to attempt to control change by limiting options. Seeking scalability may cause organizations to freeze certain aspects of their technology or approach, and subsequently find that their market has moved on and left no forwarding address—sound the violins.

The dominant market player has a vested interest in the status quo. To own a market is a highly lucrative and coveted position. No one can touch you. Or can they? Actually, being a market leader is a very vulnerable position to hold, as you have the responsibility to keep moving not only your organization upward, but the entire industry. In fact, those following the market leader may have the advantage—the benefit of second sight.

It is both costly and scary to contemplate the organizational backlash that occurs when a new competitor (see iPad) bounds into your market space and changes the customer's mindset to render your products obsolete. Your organization is then left with a warehouse full of binders, telephones, cassette tapes, and very little capacity for spin.

Science makes our lives better and miserable at the same time.

Better, because things are always improving; miserable, because they are always changing, and change can cause people a great amount of distress.

One of the most significant dilemmas organizations face is how to keep evolving and still maintain their core.

> You're on Mars, your spaceship is broken and you've forgotten your special wrench!
>
> No worries. Just print it.
>
> Z Corporation has recently developed a 3-D printer that will help you "print" the tools you need, on the planet where you need them most!
>
> +

Harnessing your science to your religion is a key way to help employees see changes in relation to their line-of-sight and remember *why* we go through it all—to improve the customer's experience and end results.

+ + +

SPACE: OUR FINAL FRONTIER.

In a MacroCultural sense, the space program ushered in a time of prosperity and hope and has become a kind of poster child for the opposite—hopelessness and struggle.

Internal issues of financial management aside, the space program was an important symbol of American belief in science, which has all but disappeared from view.

In the early sixties, John F. Kennedy positioned the space program in competition with the Russians. Thus the Space Race became an American passion and proving ground, central to the growth experienced in the 1970s and thirty years hence.

Taken from the perspective of science, the space program was an undeniable success that inspired and fostered incredible outcomes. The innovations and discoveries resulting from the space program are virtually inestimable.

But we would argue that the space program's contribution to the MacroCulture's religion was even greater.

The "what we value, we can do" theme has been a cornerstone of America's culture since its inception. Tiny, disorganized, and poorly equipped colonies versus the great British Empire not only prevailed, but also founded their own thriving nation. Upon every historical juncture, America has seen itself as capable of doing whatever necessary to succeed. This religion led to the nation's self-confidence that propelled America through the following centuries' hardships.

The space program itself came at a troublesome time, when the definition of greatness needed to be proven once again, and the formation of the space race created science as the new playing field. On July 20th 1969 our crowning achievement—the moon landing—was watched by the entire nation. The television reception was fuzzy in our drive-ins, burger shops, living rooms, and manufacturing plants, but we were glued to the screen nonetheless. Ask anyone over the age of fifty, and they will remember where they were at that moment, in the same way they will remember where they were when JFK was assassinated 6 years earlier.

The national religion (we can do anything we have a mind to) blossomed with this achievement, leading huge numbers of young people to science—the engine of our success.

Arguably, much has been lost to the MacroCulture over the interceding years. With the uncertain economic environment, our current MacroCulture is bombarded day to day with failures. At the time of this writing, we have approximately 14 million Americans unemployed and a conservative estimate would be more than double that underemployed.

College graduates with advanced degrees are finding it difficult to gain work in their fields. A young female we know who studied aerospace engineering is regularly challenged by well-intentioned people to "think about your future opportunities," which is a euphemism for reminding her the space program is not a realistic option. This is symptomatic of our wavering faith.

> **More than an embarrassment . . .**
>
> Is what William Bennet,[29] former Secretary of Education called American students scoring 23rd in math and 31st in science in comparison to 65 other top industrial countries.
>
> While the US "led the way in space after Sptunik" the decline in math and science is a threat to our national economic well-being, it is a "disaster in the making."

What is needed for successful culture is both science and religion. We cannot sustain ourselves with one or the other. Eventually, religion is pressed to "prove it," and that proof is always performance.

If we were talking about an organization, our advice would be to invest in science and use performance as a benchmark to increase confidence and create the opportunities for the growth of its people in the areas that matter most. You can't achieve excellence by squeezing the middle.

Cost-cutting without vision and hope truncates our passion and drive.

We need to dream big to ignite the positive energy of our people and connect that passion to purpose.

THE CARNIVORES VERSUS THE HERBIVORES
ORGANIC GROWTH IS THE MUSIC OF HIGH-PERFORMANCE CULTURES.

The distinguishing characteristic of high-performing organizations lies in the cultural tenets that shape their growth. High-performance cultures have sustainable and lasting growth, not the frenetic, short-term focus so popular during the past few decades. Even business giants have become symbolic ghost towns, mere shapes of what they once were.

Organizations that buy growth through acquisitions have traveled a rocky road. Why? Their strategy has produced *less* than the sum of its parts, that's why.

> In a global study of mergers and acquisitions over the past decade it was found that an organization's revenues didn't increase commensurately when two or more organizations merged, but resulted in a significant loss of the total.[30]

There are many reasons for a merger, among them dominance in the marketplace, neutralizing the competition, or developing an economy of scale. Yet many of the conventional ways organizations have tried to buy growth have backfired in the long run. Much of the blame goes to culture.

At first glance, combining the strengths of two cultures would appear to be manageable, particularly since the survivors in both organizations would seemingly have incentive to cooperate. It stands to reason that if the goals were shared, both parties could objectively partner together to achieve them. This looks great on paper.

Not so in practice. One leader shared her reflections on a recent merger between two very distinct organizations, one of which was described as "brutally competitive" and the other as "highly collaborative."

> On the day of the merger, over six hundred consultants across the globe were called together on a global teleconference where Jay, the new president, and Del, the CEO, would describe the vision for the combined organizations and calm the troops. As usual, at the end of the call they said they'd open the line for questions and one courageous (and somewhat sarcastic) consultant spoke up.

> "Yes, I have a question. How do you think the carnivores will do with the herbivores? "

Laughter was followed by a pause that turned into a few seconds of uncomfortable silence and then both parties went back to the script.

The inevitable clash of two cultures begins to sap the energy of the newly merged entity.

Any family that's attempted a merger—call it a second marriage with half-raised children—can tell you that combining cultures can take a little bit of elbow grease. As people struggle to find their new place in an organization, which has two separate and distinct histories, they are forced to reconsider their own beliefs and traditions and consider new perspectives in the name of peace and prosperity.

Independent research suggests that this loss of energy and momentum can negatively affect these organizations far into the future.[31]

Simply combining two organizations does not create a mutual culture. Often, it incites dogmatism around each culture's way.

As each separate culture struggles to hold on to their way, their people, and their view, the game of trade-off begins in earnest. It becomes a case of you keep your sales guy but we get to keep our marketing rep, we'll use your operations plan but our budgeting process, and the focus veers away from performance.

A publicly traded human resource consulting organization, RapidGroCo, grew by acquiring its competition: the companies, their products and services, and clientele. Its internal structure was redundant and its culture was fractured and local. When the marketplace shifted, RapidGroCo was unable to quickly adapt to keep pace with it.

What should have been a quick, surgical shift by its key players turned into an ill-conceived slash through its workforce.

Talented people were laid off, draining confidence from their members and stalling their momentum. Their growth, largely purchased, was poorly thought out faux-growth, not the sustainable growth of a true green culture.

Savvy leaders have long recognized the importance of culture in the process of acquiring growth through acquisition.

Kenneth Freeman, former Chairman and CEO of Quest Diagnostics, reported that in every acquisition the very first company attribute he reviewed (prior to even the financial statement) was the culture. Did

> *it marry up to the current Quest Diagnostics culture? Where would complementary partnerships exist?*

This is an example of buying growth, but only to build growth from the new culture. Buying growth and building growth combined has shown unusual success. When Ken Freeman became CEO in 1995, the market capitalization of Quest Diagnostics was $350 million. When he left in 2004, it was recorded at $9 billion-plus.

But in most cases, we are buying a numbers increase to show Wall Street or investors and don't give a hoot about the real consequences or opportunities that these assets once had at their fingertips.

Q: What are the defining attributes of a culture built for long-term growth and sustainability?
A: The growth is happening at a cellular level:

- *Its people are growing and developing.*
- *There's a shared confidence and optimism—a can-do attitude.*
- *Innovation is alive (spontaneously occurring) within work units and individuals.*

This means that products and services are improving, and, as a result, the customers are satisfied and successful. In turn, market share and customer loyalty are deepening.

Cellular level growth recharges the energy of the organization and promotes sustainability and future growth because the people themselves are consciously connected to its customers and agenda.

Growth that occurs at the expense of the cellular level is short-term, non-sustainable, and a signal that the top of the curve is nearing. Why? Because when the people become a commodity to be used up, the organization's energy is depleted. But when they are treated like an asset to be enriched, strengthened, and developed, that energy source is continually renewed.

> *Longtime New York Yankees manager Billy Martin could get results; that was certain. But his coaching expended the energy of the team, and he failed to build the future bench, leaving the team completely spent in the process. After Martin left, with the key players gone, the Yankees were forced to rebuild from scratch.*

> *In contrast, Tom Osborne, longtime football coach at the University of Nebraska, invested in the young players he recruited, developing them across the board with hard scores to focus their improvements:*

strength-building, speed, and athletics. His long-view approach yielded strong results over nearly two decades of college football.

When growth occurs from outside (acquisition), the culture reacts to the change by putting out fires rather than producing growth.

Depending on leadership to deliver growth from the top is like pushing string.
Organic growth reflects incremental steps taken throughout the organization—at every level—that create a cumulative and sustainable value to the customer.

Organic growth isn't sexy, but it is essential to survival. On second thought, it is kind of sexy.

✦ ✦ ✦

THE ESSENCE OF YOUR LEADERSHIP
IT'S FASHIONED BY THE CHOICES MADE DAY TO DAY.

Here's one of the most insightful questions we have asked leaders:

If you could do something today to change your organization, what would you do?

A great question doesn't predetermine any particular response and encourages the leader's own framework to emerge.

We think it's a useful reminder to all managers and leaders. Audible or not, each day you are effectively faced with this question as you head into work (whether that is in a downtown office building or a space in your home or head).

Leadership isn't about your track record or your educational credentials or resume, but in the select actions you take - or don't take- moment by moment.

We are frightfully fond of a phrase used extensively in retail businesses: *People vote with their feet.* If your customers don't like the service, the food, or the merchandise (on your website or in your store), they simply don't come back. From the leadership perspective, our phrase might be coined *Leaders set the tone with their own.*

As leaders, we must balance the rational with the emotional by getting involved, face-to-face with the culture; it is not enough to determine the strategy, vision, and expectations. We must be deeply curious about how our people perceive their environment. This is the reality check for our plan.

✦ ✦ ✦

THE COWBOY IN THE BOARD ROOM
CAN YOU HANDLE THE TRUTH?

We have two kinds of friends, and their vacations invariably reflect their personal orientation to life. One group says:

> *If you want to make the most of your journey, invest in the best guide you can find and follow the guide's advice.*

The other insists:

> *Exploring on your own is the only way to experience new horizons.*

Some people are real cowboys about their work—accustomed to going it alone. They feel a sense of accomplishment from plunging in and figuring things out on their own. Sometimes they buy a book or Google a resource, but they don't naturally reach out for help from others, the way they perhaps should.

> *It takes most students four years to earn an undergraduate degree; for many, it takes five or more—Super Seniors. We know a young woman, Jean, who picked up a college catalogue and proceeded to complete her BA in two-and-a-half years with no academic advice along the way.*
>
> *Later in life, Jean admits she might have "missed a few things" during her head-down marathon.*

In contrast to the cowboys, traditionalists rely upon experience for their insight and intelligence. They are continually looking for teachers or coaches. They have an innate appreciation for experience and are almost always asking, "Where have you done that before?" In selecting people for their staff, they want individuals who have "done it before" and "in this market" with "these kinds of clients."

These two styles characterize many of us, but in the executive boardrooms, the cowboy usually runs the show. But even cowboys can catch a cold;

the cowboys tend to resist seeking help, relying instead upon their hand-selected team (the "in" group) for counsel.

In life, there are plenty of trips we can take alone, figuring things out as we go. But if time is running short and importance is running high, it makes sense to seek the right assistance. Plus, there are some things that are just too risky to do yourself—like eye surgery and murder trials.

Executive team meetings are a place where risks run high, so an insightful guide makes sense. Not a guide to show you *where* to go, but rather to help you get a little perspective about where you've been and the rate of speed, performance, and casualties accrued along the way.

Contrary to what you might think, eye-rolling is not an exclusively teenage phenomenon; we've seen surreptitious eye gesticulations around many an oval table.

> *In one executive team, the animosity between two of the players, Matt and Jon, represented a serious rift that channeled its way throughout the organization. In the room, the two rarely agreed on any course of action or analysis. Whenever Matt spoke, Jon and his team would either spar or nonverbally check out. Their respective teams (sales and HR) were barely civil. The division between Matt and Jon was blocking the improvement efforts of leadership and their respective departments.*

Whenever a group convenes, the patterns of interaction tend to become relatively predictable. The family dinner table, the PTA committee, the church committee, and the quality team, all share the same tendencies; people tend to take sides and entrench themselves. The results aren't fruitful.

However, it's hard for people to recognize their own patterns; it's always easier to point fingers.

In the case above, the CEO was a part of the problem; the two warring factions each reported directly to him, and both were essential to the organization. His failure to act produced a systemic problem that was not as obvious to the CEO as it was to the other team members and their staff.

Sometimes it's helpful to bring in an outside perspective. Sometimes all you need is a reference point to add context to the situation.

An organization's ability to accept constructive feedback is a reflection of leadership. These decisions trickle into the culture. Is your culture setting the expectation for straight talk?

Can your culture handle the truth?

Each organization's relationship to the truth permeates the MacroCulture. An organization that values truth is open to alternative viewpoints. Often in the workplace, the only real independent viewpoint comes from the outside.

The best consultants help by reflecting back some of these patterns to help encourage the group to function more effectively. While there are usually a number of very talented *internal* consultants within most organizations, their perspective is often mitigated by their personal roles or stake holds in the organization. In the process of discussing specific recommendations, one VP of HR stressed the importance of taking our message directly to the executive team:

> *"It would be helpful for you to highlight that recommendation in your executive presentation; we have been pointing this issue out over the past year, but they [the senior team] need to hear it from you."*

The problems are two-fold for internal consultants: (1) The inherent difficulties in perceiving your own culture in an objective way, and (2) having your voice heard beyond your specific role and function. For these reasons, the external consultant can be highly beneficial.

Fighting with the consultant versus letting the consultant decide.

It is odd how many people pay for an expert opinion, but then do nothing with it. Individuals will see their doctor about their health, pay for the tests, and get the results. Once done, they continue to smoke, fail to exercise, and consume copious amounts of cholesterol. It begs the question: Why bother?

On the other extreme end of the continuum are those who abdicate their own responsibility and blindly follow recommendations they instinctively know are questionable. If things don't turn out right, they blame the messenger or consultant: "You told me to!"

Perhaps our least favorite are those who elect to fight their consultant over every recommendation, arguing that their perspective is better. This is akin to hiring an Impressionist to paint your portrait and then arguing about each color and brush stroke.

What are the best ways to use consultants, coaches, managers, and mentors?

Let them have their say. Hear the full idea before objecting with the detail. The merit in brainstorming is attributable to the separation of creation and evaluation, yet often people can't wait for the entire thought before they begin to correct it.

Our research indicates that the stronger the talent of the leader, the better he or she utilizes consultants. It takes a strong ego to suspend judgment when you are the ultimate decision-maker. Marginal leadership is threatened by a differing point of view and often kills the idea before it can grow enough to make a difference.

These same qualities make a difference in the management and development of people. If your leaders and managers can't let people find their own way—or pose an alternative, even radical, viewpoint—the ability of the organization to innovate, develop, and grow is severely compromised.

Let the contrary thought have its way to challenge long-standing preconceived notions. Thoughts, like books, aren't inherently dangerous, so there is very little need to burn them or the people who speak them!

✦ ✦ ✦

AFTER FOUR DECADES OF EMPLOYEE SURVEYS, THE FINAL QUESTION IS: ARE YOU LISTENING?

Managers and leaders have been the recipients of training and development that emphasized checking in or verifying what they have heard. "Now, what I hear you saying is that you agree that the report is necessary, but that you don't know how to run the report…"

Thank you, Carl Rogers; we have even mastered "How does that make you feel?"[32]

But—like the family whose home was lost in the fire and who was asked by a reporter, "And how does losing all your precious pictures and mementos make you feel?"—we are speechless, outraged, and sad. It is obvious that the reporter doesn't really care how the person feels—he is only looking for a sound bite.

The real test for great listening is that the speaker feels understood.

The manager is concerned with getting his point across. The associate's primary concern is feeling understood.

We obsess over our own clarity; we tend to overlook whether or not the other person feels understood.

Much of the time we operate within a preconceived notion that it is our role to solve the person's problem, or give them direction or guidance, or even to anticipate what they may be concerned about. This type of listening can make us semi-active in the process and on the surface gives us the feeling that we are really doing our job, but it rarely leads to the communicator feeling understood.

Organizations' efforts to understand their associates have been largely procedural: introducing the employee survey. Using engagement surveys as a vehicle provides an opportunity to understand what *they* are trying to say. Like any communication, the listening misses the mark when organizations fail to deliver—or even discuss—results. When leaders ask associates to help by providing feedback, the leaders have a commensurate obligation to discuss the results so that people feel understood. If the leaders can't or won't follow through, then they shouldn't ask for the feedback.

Organizations are successful when their people feel understood. Anything less is falling short.

Employee surveys have absorbed copious amounts of organizational energy over the past four decades, all in the interest of helping people feel heard—

or understood. In fact, they are the leading vehicle for organizational feedback, from leadership's perspective. As such, we are taking a deep dive into the world of survey research, from its promise to delivery.

+ + +

TESTING...TESTING...TESTING...

In the not too distant past, people living with diabetes had to visit their physician to test their blood glucose levels. Yet, blood glucose varies throughout the day, so periodic testing provides little ability to manage the disease. With the advent of technology to track blood glucose at any moment during the day, diabetics have gained control over the disease. Instead of visiting the doctor weekly for a test and waiting for the prescribed action, if a diabetic has low levels, he or she can simply eat an apple.

> ### HOW WE TEST = WHAT WE KNOW = WHAT WE CAN DO ABOUT IT
>
> Effective management of diabetes depends on three different metrics:
>
> - Blood Glucose Level = moment-to-moment variability = immediate management
>
> - Fructosamine (short-term control of blood glucose levels over the past 1-3 weeks) = compliance to goals and priorities = focused management.
>
> - Hemoglobin A1c (average blood glucose levels over 1-4 months) = long range compliance and impact = long term management.
>
> This is a pretty insightful metaphor for organizations, as well.
>
> 1) Moment by moment you manage culture in touchpoints.
>
> 2) These touchpoints accumulate into months of energy and productivity or the lack thereof.
>
> 3) At least once a year, measuring the trend (gain or loss) in energy clarifies your progress to goals.
>
> + + +

Consider how much energy is saved when diabetics can diagnose their own levels compared to being dependent on outside sources?

In an ideal world, organizations would monitor engagement and energy levels continuously, just like people with diabetes. Instead, they are stuck in a system that resembles an annual doctor's visit.

Engagement surveys are often delayed by leadership's unwillingness to have their organization's state captured for perpetuity. The most common reason provided is that "We know there are problems due to x, y, or z"—restructuring or changes in the benefit package, usually—"making this a very bad time to survey."

Not measuring employee engagement when times are bad is equivalent to not balancing your checkbook on a bad month.
If you take your temperature when you have a fever, does knowing the number make the fever worse?

Once the surveys have been conducted and the engagement levels mapped, at-risk areas can be identified. Given what is known about the relationship between engaged people and customers, productivity, retention, and growth, it is no stretch to view some work-unit scores as a 911 call for help. The point of the measurement is to give the leader or manager an opportunity to self-correct, to step in quickly and lessen the drag on productivity and prevent further decline or loss.

In the world of engagement measurement and employee satisfaction, the process itself lost its distinction and power to improve performance long ago. This is partially because the process is no longer novel and partially because the process has never transcended from an *event* to the self-corrective tool it was meant to be.

> *A hospital we'll call Samaritan Health was caught in the uncomfortable position of needing to perform their annual engagement survey before the work-group discussions and action plans from their last survey had been completed.*

> *This nine-month delay meant that women who were not pregnant when they first took the survey had already given birth before they had the opportunity to see their scorecards for engagement.*

In this case, the work groups at risk were long past expecting their 911 calls to be answered. That was pretty much a blue-ribbon lesson in *this data no longer applies.*

Compelling evidence exists that holding onto poor results is one of the worst things an organization can do. So much so, that one CEO we know recently coined a new approach for his organization: *Bad News Fast.*

Engagement is a state and not a trait.

It describes a transitory context.

When the situation changes, so do levels of energy and commitment.

Believing problems will solve themselves is wishful thinking; things can, and often do, get worse.

How often do people slide from actively engaged to passenger status because their feedback doesn't solve the problem? Our data suggests it's more common than not, particularly when we violate the expectations of others.

In its basic form, an employee survey is a promise extended to associates.

It says we (the leaders and managers of this organization) care about you (our employees) and want you to respond (to the survey items) so we can know your perceptions (of this organization, your immediate work environment, and management). Implicit in that promise is that if you take the survey, we will consider your viewpoint and do something (hopefully positive) in response to improve our organization and your livelihood. In its abbreviated form:

If you do X (respond), we promise to do Y (make something good happen).

X is clear, but Y leaves plenty of room for interpretation.

WHAT IS Y? FIGURING OUT LEADERSHIP'S SIDE OF THE DEAL.

While most managers want to see their team members highly engaged at work, enjoying what they do and the contributions they make, when the survey results are returned, the information often feels very personal to the manager. In spite of the organization's eagerness to do better, the human reaction is denial:

Is this really accurate?

I don't think my team understood this item.

Work schedules had to be switched around last month and people were mad...

Why is denial such a common reaction to surveys and other organizational dilemmas?

Because it works. Once we explain away the reason, the results are far less painful.

Managers who feel uncomfortable with the survey results have a tendency to explain what the results *mean* to team members, who were the very people who provided the feedback!

That said, what are the best ways to overcome these natural feelings and fulfill the survey promise? Y, done right, means three things: discussing results, demonstrating positive changes, and keeping the conversation alive from survey to survey.

Discuss results by asking people what they mean.

Research shows that when organizations thoroughly discuss engagement results, their associates report significantly higher levels of engagement on the following year's survey.

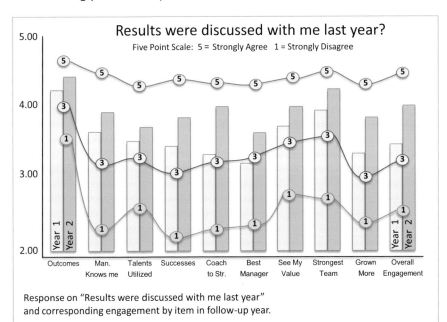

Response on "Results were discussed with me last year" and corresponding engagement by item in follow-up year.

The gray bars reflect two years of client data across nine items. The bars on the far right of the graph reflect the overall engagement score. The graph shows three groups based on their response to the following item: *The prior year's survey results were discussed with me and my team.* The green-5-line depicts the responses of employees who reported that they *had* discussed the engagement results (5 = strongly agreed), and the red-1-line reflects all employees who reported that they *had not* discussed the results (1 = strongly disagreed). Clearly, the results suggest that if every MicroCulture (working unit) had discussed the survey results, engagement scores in year 2 would have been much higher across the organization.[33]

The best team meetings are those that provoke dialogue and discussion. The manager doesn't have to position himself as an expert, with all the answers, but he must demonstrate commitment by asking open-ended questions and listening. We can't know what the results actually mean until our people tell us, in the same way that we can't know how people really feel unless they choose to share that with us.

People need to see positive changes resulting from the survey process.

The second key to improvement requires that people see positive changes result from their feedback. It is not the size of the change that matters; it

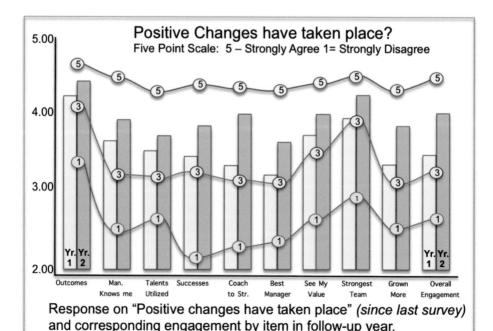

Response on "Positive changes have taken place" *(since last survey)* and corresponding engagement by item in follow-up year.

is the origin of the change. Whose idea was it? To whom does it matter? When change is initiated in response to team feedback and discussion, the change is owned by the group, and defined as positive. The graph below demonstrates the impact of positive changes on the future engagement of work teams.

As in the previous graphic, the overall engagement of the organization is shown across two years; the red-1 and green-5 lines reflect groups that were formed based on their response to the following item: *"Last year's survey resulted in positive changes."*

The green-5-line reflects the engagement level of those who strongly agreed that the survey resulted in positive changes; the red-1-line reflects the engagement level of employees who strongly disagreed with this statement.

We have seen these patterns repeated almost without exception in every organization with which we have worked. People do not expect the world, but they do expect leaders to fulfill the promise extended as a part of the survey process.[34]

Keep the conversation going from survey to survey.

The final element is keeping engagement alive throughout the year. For initiative-weary associates, the typical engagement survey process is an effort in futility. The following graphic demonstrates the problem associated with making engagement an *event* and not a way of life. The amount of energy and focus required to implement the survey completely overshadows the value of the feedback.

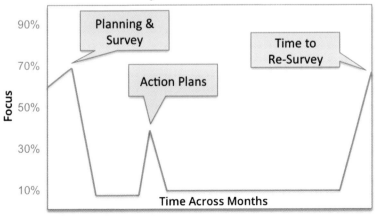

Traditional Approach, *Activity (focus) across Time*

Having shown this figure[35] to hundreds of executives and HR leaders, we have yet to find anyone who didn't flinch, admitting to the truth of the situation. Like other significant initiatives that involve team members, we tend to be much better in the planning and directing than in the involving and sustaining. Follow-up (if any) tends to be more procedural than helpful, also known as the action planning process.

+ + +

IS FILING THE ONLY ACTION RESULTING FROM YOUR ACTION PLANNING PROCESS?

In the interest of encouraging manager accountability, action planning has emerged as the new survey standard. Like all such initiatives, it was born with the best intentions, manufactured to solve the problems associated with poor manager follow-up.

Action planning has become the latest energy-consumer in the engagement world. It appears to drain more energy from the manager and team than it returns in results.

In fact, the majority of the activity generated around the action planning process is the manager completing and submitting the form. It's become like copying your friend's math homework in the hallway five minutes before class begins.

An engagement consultant described his experience with the process:

> We had just completed a manager forum with an organization when the VP of HR received the first of the action plans back via e-mail from Garth, one of the senior production managers. We reviewed the carefully completed plan, submitted only minutes after the survey results had been sent to Garth. We were stunned to realize that in spite of the training and countless messages to the contrary, he had completely skipped discussing the results with his team.
>
> When questioned, Garth explained that the meeting wasn't necessary, as he understood exactly what the data meant and what to do about it.

Providing managers with a form to complete triggers the following response: *What's the quickest way to get this done?*

The good news is that's usually what we want from our management team—quick action and delivery of results. The bad news is that this is counterproductive when the subject is employee engagement. In employee engagement, the journey that managers take with their team members is the only path to sustainable results. An action plan is not the result we are looking for, even though organizations tend to keep score on these plans as if they were.

Employee data is not about fixing problems, it is about continuing the conversation around how we work to maximize our effectiveness.

Managers often rush to the completion of the plan and forget the conversation, which is the true meat and potatoes of change.

The moves we make to encourage the manager to be accountable should be slight nuances, not blatant wholesale attempts to saddle them with procedural accountability. What is the real test for our managers? Associate engagement.

Farewell action plan. Make way for results.

+ + +

CELEBRATING PROGRESS IS FAR MORE USEFUL THAN PLANNING ACTION

As we have discussed, energy is ignited or drained in the MicroCultures and heavily dependent upon the immediate manager and team. This energy is most often measured via the engagement survey process and reported back at all levels of leadership: local, departmental, and overall.

Whose job is it to insure results? Organizations struggle to see results from their engagement surveys largely because the process is shared across the culture.

Traditionally, leaders *preside* over the survey process. They are decision-makers about timing, scope, and the questions asked. Often they are rule-makers with respect to action plans and follow-up requirements. It's a dignified, pristine role. But, unfortunately, their distance from the process limits their involvement.

Leaders need to get dirty.

To insure the process really delivers the needed results, leaders must work directly with their managers and supervisors, around three fundamentals:

1) Start the conversation.
2) Do something based on the feedback.
3) Celebrate and repeat.

Let's take a closer look at how leaders can work with their managers to bring these fundamentals to life.

+ + +

STARTING THE CONVERSATION

When survey results come back to the organization, the manager feels the pressure—and so does the team. Ideally, the manager shares and discusses the findings, and remains open to the input of the team.

In actual practice, this often plays out more like a presentation than a conversation among friends and partners. Worse, it may be the only time the team considers the results.

Our research suggests that thinking about this as a conversation is more helpful to managers. Conversations are multidirectional and flow with the interest and input of the participants. Nobody knows where it will end up, because the ultimate destination is a product of the participants' interaction, not a predetermined spot.

> "The survey results have told us that people don't feel that their opinions count here.
>
> As a reminder, we have had an open door policy for over two years. If you are not taking advantage of it, it's not our problem."
>
> -COO

The spontaneous nature of a conversation releases pressure.

Managers spontaneously start and stop conversing throughout the day about the work itself— Will you have that report for me today? Do we have enough steak cut for the evening shift? They naturally pick up conversations where they left off. That same conversational muscle needs to be exercised around how we work together:

How is the second shift working out? Are there some things that could make it go more smoothly? What ideas do you have? How can I help?

The best managers approach the entire feedback session more like a student than a director.

They are anxious to hear what people are thinking, and that is what makes their people feel understood. When people feel understood, they want to help.

Of course, it takes more than just a word like conversation to make an impact. Once the conversation starts, the most successful managers and leaders can make it ongoing.

So how do leaders really insure that these conversations are spontaneously happening? By starting their own conversations with each of their managers, demonstrating their interest in how the manager's work is progressing—from the survey to the end result. Like the best managers, the most successful leaders keep the conversations going, keeping the focus on engaging the hearts and minds of their people.

The distance between us is reduced through conversation.

What will we do differently as a result of this conversation?

> So we did the survey...so what? Nothing will change. It never has before.

How do we convince people that this time is different? That this time we really will do something as a result of our conversation?

For the past decade, we have posed this question to thousands of managers in many different venues:

How many of you have participated in an employee survey?

Nearly every hand goes in the air.

How many of you have had an outstanding experience?

No hands go up.

One manager, put it eloquently:

I have taken engagement surveys for 30 years and have never seen anything positive come out of them!

+

We don't convince by trying to "fix things" based on the survey. Managers are not solely responsible for engagement; it can't be done without the associates and their inherent desire to contribute.

We convince people by involving them in defining what needs to change and why. The people themselves are the change. The most successful managers both encourage action from others and take action themselves.

That means more than a team meeting—it means an individual approach. We have reviewed the universal needs of people at work, things like:

- *Seeing the value of our contribution to the organization and its customers;*
- *Using and developing our talents and capabilities; and*
- *Having supportive relationships with our manager and team members.*

Great managers work with each individual to build a close, supportive relationship to uncover the individual's unique strengths, capabilities, and dreams. Being deeply interested in each person helps the manager fine-tune the role to the person.

It is often these small, individual changes that lead to people feeling understood and believing in the process.

What can leadership do? First, recognize that many of the changes that will make the difference in the MicroCulture are not the stuff of the typical action plan. The changes that matter tend to be personal, individual, and emerge through authentic conversations between managers and team members and within the team itself.

The leadership equivalent would be one-on-one conversations with each manager on their own team, making it a point to uncover with that person what makes a difference in his work life each and every day, where they want to grow, and how the leader can offer support.

+ + +

CELEBRATE SUCCESS. THEN REPEAT.

Celebration is highly underrated. Nothing drives results upward like success, so why not celebrate? A win is inspiring; it reinforces our faith in our own power to improve circumstances.

Most communication patterns revolve around problems rather than successes. Some groups (social, work, family) tend to move from problem to problem as an operating focus. If there isn't a problem, the meeting isn't really necessary.

People often forget to celebrate incremental successes, but progress is what encourages people through obstacles.

> *Research with the most effective nurses revealed their unique abilities to perceive the increments of improvement in the health of their patients. Once communicated to patient and family, this accelerated the patient's healing.*

> *Research with outstanding teachers suggests they are able to identify glimpses of excellence unique to their students and that the teacher's recognition of that excellence with the students serves as a catalyst to the students' learning.*

The action planning process has historically made little fuss about success and is front-loaded relative to planning. Managers should turn their attention from planning to celebration.

Leadership's role must be attentiveness to success. If leaders don't notice the successes, what's the point of ever pushing our limits? Wins excite us; they produce energy.

In response to our recommendation to "celebrate success", a struggling organization confessed:

> *We have nothing to celebrate. . .*

When the small wins go unnoticed, the larger ones get even more unlikely.

SUCCESS BUILDS CONFIDENCE

Employees who experience positive changes, have significantly higher confidence in leadership.

Their confidence results more from their belief in the leader's ability to make the right things happen, than from the official vision or direction.

Coffman Research Institute, 2012, Vol 4:2.

Problem cultures—where nothing is ever celebrated—destroy optimism and hope, ultimately stripping the passion from work.

Leaders can stop this cycle by asking, "What's going right around here?"

It should be apparent that to get more of something, we need to give more of that same thing. This is the leadership challenge. We get more engaging managers when we engage with the managers.

IT'S THURSDAY, 10 A.M.
DO YOU KNOW HOW ENGAGED YOUR WORKFORCE IS?

Just as cell phones have made all us amateur photographers and reporters, today's information technology connects us all simultaneously. We can literally review the same data and watch the same trends live, as the organization posts gains and losses real-time.

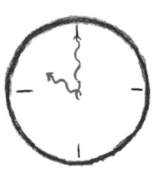

How does this change the way we work together?

As individuals, we stubbornly hold on to our ways longer than our technology holds on in our organization.

We have the raw capacity for change quicker than we have the stomach for it.

Most management practices have their feet firmly planted in the past.

We've all heard the adage: The learning begins when the student arrives. In contrast, the technology usually arrives while management is still pressing the snooze button.

Let's revisit the outcomes we are looking to achieve.

1) **Executive teams need hard results.** Feelings are fine, but if we can't connect the dots to performance, then the executive team won't get their heads in the game. The numbers must connect to outcomes of significance: customer loyalty, per person productivity, margin/sales, and human performance.

2) **People need to believe their leader's motives are authentic,** that their talent, focus, creativity, and energy are highly valued every day of the year, not just at survey time. The only way for them to know this is when our touchpoints with them demonstrate that their ideas, feelings, and point of view *really are* that important and we *really are* committed to them.

3) **Managers need to understand that the survey is not a personal scorecard, but an energy gauge,** which communicates productive versus wasted energy of our most precious assets, our people. You

can't drive from Minneapolis to Chicago on half a tank of gas. Employee engagement is not another initiative, but an implicit way of managing people inseparable from every other strategic move we make in the name of customers or business results.

4) **People need to own their role process.** Providing ongoing education, conversation, and support for the entire organization (leaders, managers, and associates) would deliver on our promise: to engage each person in the process of building a highly productive place to work, where everyone on the team has a clear line-of-sight to our customer.

If we could re-engineer our engagement process from this vantage point, what would it look like?

It's 10 a.m., Thursday morning. Please open your phone or computer:

10:00–10:05—Every associate takes one to two minutes to respond to the survey and sends his or her unique perspective to management.

11:00—Discovery sessions begin with associates leading the discussion: How can we build an even better place to work?

12:00-the Exec team begins a state of engagement forum, complete with the entire company's data.

It is Thursday at 1:00 p.m., and, yes, there's a score. But more importantly, the people feel understood!

+ + +

DOLLARS AND SENSE TO CULTURE
HOW FISCAL REWARDS AFFECT US.

Companies communicate values through rewards.

When a company attaches money to an outcome, they will get more of that outcome. People do what they are paid to do, so when the pay plan reinforces the wrong things, the wrong things become important.

Inappropriate or pseudo-measures distract us from the real business of developing customer loyalty.

Everyone knows it, particularly our most engaged customer service representatives. Here's a story from a top performing customer service representative:

> *"In my company, we are supposed to respond to a customer call and fix the problem in a certain period of time. That's how we are rated and bonused. But if an elderly customer calls or anyone who has a difficult time explaining things, you know then that that call will exceed your allotted time.*
>
> *One of my coworkers is known for being a top performer in our department. As soon as she gets a call like this, she just disconnects the customer. The customer calls back in and gets someone else, and she ends up with really high scores and high pay, month after month."*

Don't you hate it when they "accidentally" cut you off right after you've explained your problem? All along, we thought it was our bad luck! Who knew it was by design?

You might think that paying people by activity would be the equivalent of paying for performance, but that kind of reasoning often causes people to neglect the real outcomes.

> *An executive team determined that engagement was so important they would distribute bonuses to teams that achieved high scores on their engagement survey. Naturally, all of the employees began reporting higher engagement scores, but the results didn't reflect any actual improvement.*

Money is certainly critical to motivation, but research suggests it doesn't necessarily improve performance. To properly align motivation and compensation, it is important to observe the individual's relationship to money. Our research identified the following recurring types of relationships:

5) **Hard need:** "I need more money." A certain level of compensation is essential for the security and safety of the individual's family.

6) **Worth:** "My money measures my worth." Money is how this person measures success; it is tangible evidence that their contribution is valued.

7) **Fairness:** "In comparison to _____, my compensation isn't fair." This is about perceived fairness, so it's always relative to others (colleagues, bosses, and staff).

WHAT ARE THE WORST WAYS TO MOTIVATE PEOPLE WITH MONEY?

1. Tell employees the $$$ is not about them. It is all about the norms of other companies – and don't tell them what companies.

2. Tell them the $$$ is "all we can afford" – then get in your Mercedes and drive home.

3. Let them know that no matter how good they are, they will only make $$$ at this job because that's all the job is worth.

4. Tell them everyone will make the same bonus.

5. Don't tell them how you are evaluating them, but tell them that $$$ is based on performance.

6. When it is time to review their performance, skip it and tell them it really doesn't matter – they are doing "just fine".

7. Change the way you evaluate their performance right before their bonus is due.

8. Be vague about the benefits.

9. When you mention promotional opportunities, always work in the phrase "over the years" in the conversation.

10. When they ask about $$$, change the subject to something that is "more important at this time".

+ + +

All of these needs are valid. People make short-term choices when their income cannot comfortably support their family.

Executive action affects perceptions of fairness; if the executive team's bonus increases while employee benefits and financial rewards are curtailed, the incongruity doesn't seem fair. In contrast, when executives make clear their values with respect to compensation, the organization stays on track. As one executive described it:

> "It's about the mission, not the money. In fact, management for the past three years has not taken a merit increase. Our priority is to take care of the front-line staff first."

This phrase captures the essence of a leadership team that is clearly about the mission and doesn't let its own compensation get in the way of their commitment.

Compensation has a connotative meaning which goes well beyond the dollars themselves.

Money is a metaphor for the organization's reverence of our work. What does your organization revere?

✦ ✦ ✦

SIGNS, SIGNS, EVERYWHERE A SIGN

Signs, signs, everywhere a sign

Blocking out the scenery, breaking my mind

Do this, don't do that, can't you read the sign?

In 1970, the Canadian group Five Man Electrical Band recorded the song "Signs," which began with the lyrics above. The point of the song may have been in jest; regardless, these signs have crept into our organizational cultures—from parking lots to bathrooms. Take ten steps in your workplace and count the number of signs you see.

Signs were initially invented to educate and bring people helpful information (Curve Ahead). These signs proclaiming warnings have saved countless lives. However, these friendly reminders have become like a helicopter-mom's attempt to change people's behavior. Some of these signs leave us feeling like a child.

Just prior to speaking to an executive team regarding their organization's state of engagement, I had occasion to use the facilities. They were beautiful accommodations for the purpose, with gleaming wood walls and impeccably shined fixtures. No expense had been spared to achieve the ambiance: smart and sophisticated.

Turning to leave, a sign in large bold print taped to the back of the door greeted me:

Did You
Remember
To Flush?

Returning from the bathroom, I asked the executives whom the sign was for? How many people using that washroom required a sign like that? The signs were quickly removed.

The question remains: Why do we feel compelled to legislate a rule that only applies to one percent of our workforce?

Why is it so seductive to address a problem by posting a sign? Why can't we just talk to the one or two that caused the concern in the first place? Therein lies the difference between a *Curve Ahead* sign and a *Did You Remember to Flush?* sign—the first is clearly to help the individual reading it, while the second is a way to get people to behave.

The next time you see a sign, ask yourself, is this here to help us or control us?

Why do leaders feel such a need to control employees' behavior? High-performance cultures trust that the majority of their people will do the right thing. How many signs do you have in your home to insure that your family members behave themselves?

We have noticed a correlation between the good times and challenging times in an organization and the number of signs posted. During times of fear, we feel compelled to *keep everyone in line*. Sadly, this actually minimizes people's confidence in using their intelligence, ideas, and innovative instincts—when we need them most!

If you have a problem, skip the sign and talk directly with those who need reminding.

Pay close attention to how the messages on signs make people feel. Wouldn't you prefer to post a few signs like:

Innovation Together—Right Here!

Share Customer Insights and Intelligence!

Celebration Zone

We'll Help! Bring Us Your Challenge

Most organizations manage to the lowest common denominator; great cultures develop policy around great practices.

+   +   +

LIGHTEN UP! SOMEWHERE, SOMEHOW, A DUCK IS WATCHING YOU.

Or is that a surveillance camera?

Spend eight-plus hours each day at work in ridiculous situations that have you muttering under your breath and there is only one remedy: laugh about it. Not a chuckle, but a loud, belly-rolling guffaw in which the coffee shoots right out of your nose. So it's a little undignified; you'll get over it. And when you do, it could be time to actually do something to make the situation right.

> *Laughter gives us distance. It allows us to step back from an event, deal with it, and then move on.*
> —*Bob Newhart*

We seek humor because it feels good to laugh. Laughter is good for the spirit, good for the body, and good for the morale of the team. People learn most when they are open to new experiences. It reminds us of this classic spoof:

> *A new employee is talking to the boss. The boss gets up, looks out the window, and yells, "Green side up!" Then he comes back to the desk.*
>
> *A few minutes later, he does it again. The boss repeats the sequence three times before the new employee asks what's going on.*

"I've got employees out there, laying sod."

Blog us if you have worked for this boss.

Humor can also be destructive. Even as we're laughing about something, it finds a way to change us.

When humor is at the expense of another person, a negative synergy develops.

We reduce the person with our observation, and then upon each retelling, the individual loses a bit more; when others pick up the refrain, the situation gets even worse.

We know cultures that have become toxic with this syndrome. One manager called his a "pecking culture":

> *"Have you ever seen a barnyard full of chickens? One gets a sore and the entire flock pecks at it. That's what this place is like."*

Humor that pecks away at people destroys the spirit and diminishes trust; the end result is far less than the sum of its parts.

Does humor in the workplace make us more or less effective? Does your culture laugh with people or at them?

High performance cultures laugh with people—sharing the bizarre and the ridiculous together. This extends beyond the people to the customer.

> **Tell them the story about...**
>
> How many times have you heard this from friends and co-workers? What a terrific clue to a joyful culture where people encourage each other to laugh.
>
> ✦

In contrast, when the culture is poking fun at the expense of its people or its customers, the underlying relationship is negatively affected. We found this example on one website highlighting the dangers of laughing at your customers:

> *The other day I went to sell some books. There was a separate desk in the back of the store. I brought in a bag and two clerks started sorting through them.*

Another guy lined up behind me. One of the clerks said to him, "Are you here to sell books?" "Yes," the man said. The clerk responded, "Wait in the line outside."

The guy went outside. Thirty seconds later he was back. The clerk repeated, "Wait in the line outside." "There is no line outside," the man said meekly.

The clerk sighed, looked at the other clerk, and sarcastically said, "There is no line outside." The other clerk said gruffly, "If you can't figure out the line, then you can't sell books here." The potential seller walked back outside.

A minute later, a girl walked up with books. "Wait in the line outside," said the clerk again. She walked outside. A few moments later, she was back. "What are you doing?" the clerk asked. "Selling books," she said. "The line is outside," the clerk said.

She walked outside again.

The clerks laughed. "Let's see if the Mensa society out there can figure out how the line works!" And they laughed some more, as if both these customers were complete buffoons.

Lucky for me, I had arrived moments before these other two, because I had no idea there was a place outside to wait in line! Or maybe "There's a line outside" actually means "Form a line outside"? [36]

Our MacroCulture exudes stories of awful customers, just as it overflows with stories of awful service providers. If we are content with that, our work is done. If not, there is a long trek ahead...

Highly productive culture is always an exception to the norm. Highly productive cultures don't laugh at customers—they cherish them.

✦ ✦ ✦

BELIEVERS MAKE THE BEST CUSTOMERS

We commonly hear "Those with the best players win." We agree and propose a corollary: Those with the best customers grow.

How much does a poor customer cost you? The best customers make you better, and the worst destroy your value. However, most organizations spend their energy and money trying to acquire new customers rather than new, high-quality customers.

A great customer is not an easy customer, any more than a great place to work is an easy place to work.

The most demanding customers—those who want more for their dollar, more utility from their products, greater attentiveness to their concerns— are not necessarily bad customers. Our line-of-sight to those unique concerns creates the impetus for innovation and service; these difficult customers actually make us better.

Embrace the believers, and then embrace their headache...

Some customers buy, and some customers are believers. The believers feel an intense connection to a person first and local entity second and a broader brand third. Believers see something different than regular customers do. They see the *what ifs* in you and your organization. The most meaningful encounters involve emotion, an indication the customer is seeing in 3D. They genuinely want to make you better, and, if we're honest, the believers are the authors of true innovation.

Customer headaches become organizational headaches. The process of denial tends to institutionalize the problem.

When organizations have problems they don't know how to fix, they inadvertently decide they can't be fixed.

The great brands of today have embraced customers' feedback; instead of just hoping it will go away, they ask, "How can this become a key differentiator?" One need not look further than:

"Darn, I don't have a receipt...."

    Nordstrom embraced the headache of returned merchandise.

"I want to use it—not spend all day installing it..."

    Apple combined both hardware and software.

"I give up—this will never work..."

> Apple stores put you eye to eye with a *"Genius"* to fix your problem.

"How do I get from home or work to the rental car?"

> Enterprise Rent-A-Car says, *"We pick you up."*

"How will I ever find that?"

> Google allows us to search a topic and get instant access to information. *(Remember the card files and Dewey decimal system?)*

"I hate to call for service."

> At Ritz-Carlton, the customer's problem is owned by the first person it is told to, no matter their official title.

"I'm bored with the games I have..."

> GameStop allows gamers to trade in old games for new.

Customers who help us to improve results make extraordinary partners. But customers who resist our products, advice, council, service, and representatives can make hostages of our people and diminish our culture.

The pressures to be more efficient are helpful; however, terrorists are not. And when a customer holds your people hostage, you must free them or suffer the consequences. It is counterproductive to have line-of-sight with your worst customers. Great organizations fire poor customers, rather than let them detract from their people and thus their culture and ability to compete.

The best organizations systematically build around the best customers, forming partnerships that contribute to symbiotic growth. Line-of-sight with a great customer stirs innovation in both customer and service provider.

We have seen stellar examples of customer/vendor partnership. Toyota has consistently practiced great partnership with its suppliers, even to the point of locating them adjacent to their manufacturing plants.

What constitutes a great customer? The list varies, of course, by the situation, but here are a few traits you can take to the bank:

1) Great customers don't keep you guessing. They keep educating you about their goals, needs, and dreams so you can increase your usefulness to them.

2) Great customers share your values about service to *their* customers and work alongside you to jointly develop their people and do the right thing.

3) Great customers are up front about what works and what doesn't so that you can solve problems together. They give you a chance to work with them to make things right.

4) Great customers appreciate that *both* you and they must be profitable in order to sustain the business long term. They won't begrudge you a reasonable profit margin.

The culture of an organization is extremely sensitive to its customer. The quality of the customer either provides opportunities for growth, innovation, and purpose or strangles the organization and limits the future of its members.

+ + +

SUCCESS INSPIRES GROWTH
GROWTH FEEDS SUCCESS.

A review of the Dow Jones over the past fifty years is a powerful reminder of the importance of success to culture.[37]

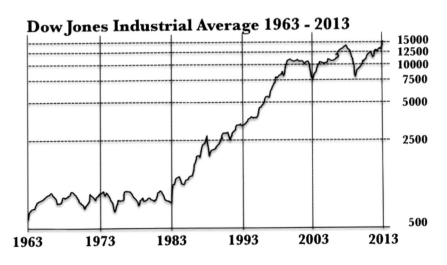

Dow Jones Industrial Average 1963 - 2013

Even the most faithful trend-followers can lose sight of the distance traveled since the mid-1970s. The ups and downs of the past few years pale in comparison to the amazing growth experienced by US organizations in the two decades between 1980 and 2000. There were losses of course, and plenty of challenges, but the MacroCulture literally burst with opportunity, and the advances made during these times both resulted from and fed that growth.

It is the growth of our organizations that provides the catalyst and focus for the growth of our people. Without opportunity, however, development and growth can become academic and esoteric, focused more on learning for its own sake than on line-of-sight to the customer. This discovery connecting personal growth to organizational growth will be an essential element for leadership over the next several decades.

Like any organism, when the MacroCulture becomes fat with growth, its focus waivers.

As a consequence, over the past thirty years of accelerated growth, our organizations, schools, and academic institutions experienced a renaissance of sorts, expanding their internal resources to match their heightened awareness of all things human. We witnessed an expansion from personnel as a support function to human resources, people strategy, talent management, and the emergence of organizational development. These were not mistakes, but they were certainly a reflection of abundance.

In the dampened economic mood, organizations are fighting for their survival, and the focus is swinging back to the essentials, chopping the branches that fail to yield sufficient fruit.

A culture born during a fight for survival cuts off the nonessential and focuses energy in areas crucial to its longevity. This is like the human body's response to threat:

> *When our fight-or-flight response is activated, sequences of nerve cell firing occur. Chemicals like adrenaline, noradrenalin, and cortisol are released*

LOOKING BACK FOR SUCCESS

In the course of interviewing thousands of managers over the past decade, we learned that for many, the past held more passion and excitement than the present. Talented leaders reached back to times of growth, energy, and innovation for their more vivid examples of success.

This is a trend we can ill afford.

into our bloodstream and cause our body to undergo a series of very dramatic changes. Our respiratory rate increases. Blood is shunted away from our digestive tract and directed into our muscles and limbs, which require extra energy and fuel for running and fighting.

Our pupils dilate. Our awareness intensifies. Our sight sharpens. Our impulses quicken. Our perception of pain diminishes. Our immune system mobilizes with increased activation. We become prepared— physically and psychologically—for fight or flight. We scan and search our environment, looking for any potential enemy.[38]

Facing extinction, our bodies become smarter about what is important for survival.

But culture doesn't respond as quickly as the human body. It lags behind, reflecting yesterday better than tomorrow.
And while people can anticipate, cultures can only react.

+ + +

MAD HATTERS
A CULTURE IN FEAR MAKES EXPENSIVE DECISIONS.

When the culture provokes feelings of insecurity, its energy is nonproductive. At critical times, when the organization most needs its people inspired and hopeful, the people are frantic and frenzied by fear.

Rick, a chief medical officer of a for-profit health care system in the Southwest, discovered that the "war of numbers" taking place during the infamous MORs (monthly operating reviews) had effectively stunned and immobilized his work force. Employees knew it wasn't safe to speak up because when financial targets were missed the reaction was punitive and blaming. Monthly budget reviews had turned into witch-hunts.

"Health-care delivery had become a mathematical equation," Rick said. He set out to get people to open up. Rich would open meetings by writing seemingly outrageous quotes on the white board, such as "Create joy, not fear" and "A scorecard is not a strategy." He knew that he was getting a reputation as a pot-stirrer, but he met with little success.

One day, in frustration, he finally resorted to humor, using a quote from Alice in Wonderland. "'But I don't want to go among mad people,' Alice

> *remarked. 'Oh, you can't help that,' said the cat. 'We're all mad here. I'm mad, you're mad, we're all mad.'"*

> *This quote seemed so accurate to his stone-faced colleagues, they nodded knowingly. A few even smiled. Slowly team members started to contribute.* "They still fall back into old habits, and they still think I'm the Mad Hatter," *says Rick,* "but at least they're talking."

People need to be able to speak the truth. If a company terminates its *truth tellers*—the employees or leaders who have the courage or insight to do the right thing—this sends a very powerful message that doing the right thing may get you fired. This message can potentially immobilize the workforce so drastically that it may take years to recover.

In a reaction to fear and change, we see people divide themselves into tribes:

> *One tribe consists of those who are fearful of the change. This tribe goes into hiding in the hopes that the company will run out of steam and things will return to normal. Then there's the skeptical tribe, waiting to see signals proving that leadership is really serious about the culture change.*

> *But the most dangerous tribe consists of silver-tongued devils, terrorists who learn the language and give lip service to the change, but all the time they are secretly working against it.*

So, in the tribal war that is cultural change, it is leadership's responsibility to manage the fear in the long-term interests of vision and growth. This means inspiring hope and confidence, encouraging truth-tellers, and simultaneously protecting the culture from terrorists within. The faint of heart need not apply.

+ + +

THE BRIDGE INSPECTION
WILL YOUR CONNECTIONS SUPPORT THE TRAFFIC?

To close the strategy gap, the organization must align the energy of its departments and groups with its singular purpose: the customer. One of leadership's challenges is to measure the efficacy of the BridgeCulture, that is, the organization's capacity for spontaneously adapting and aligning its energy to deliver superior performance.

Like the synaptic connections in our nervous system, the connections among our groups within an organization signal true synergy or its absence.

Are we consistently making our organization smarter, faster, and more effective? Or are we encouraging isolated sectors of activity?

Traditionally, organizations have used internal service measures to assess their interdepartmental effectiveness. These have often created more dissonance than insight, due to the well-intentioned yet ineffective measures and expectations. It is not uncommon to see internal service measures focus on transactional data under the guise of objectivity.

For example:

- *How many rings before a phone is answered, reflecting our team's responsiveness to other groups in the organization.*
- *It should take 23 minutes for the housekeeping department to make up a patient's room.*
- *Is our daily report delivered at 10 a.m. every day like clockwork?*

While these measurements seem clean and tidy, few actually present an authentic relationship to the desired outcomes of the business. In fact, when it comes to a hospital's readiness, all rooms are not created equally; some take more time, some are more important. Similarly, sometimes we are not able to pick up a phone because we are engaged with customers whose concerns are more urgent and reflective of our true mission and purpose. We hear great service providers complain:

> *If you are evaluating me, at least focus on the real value of my contribution and not just irrelevant tasks or activities.*

The collection of internal service data like this can cause an unfortunate residue, decreasing the partnerships among teams and between members. It fosters an us-versus-them mentality.

In terms of negative feedback—or poor data—you can't unring the bell.

Providing the wrong measures can irreparably damage the outcome we are most interested in achieving: *One team, one mission, one company.*

At the MacroCultural level, our goal is improving interdepartmental cooperation and teamwork among all the groups within our organization. How should we measure the effectiveness of our various BridgeCultures?

Our research suggests that in the most productive cultures, people recognize the reciprocal nature of their relationships. Three dimensions capture the essence of high-performing bridges:

> 1) *Partnership: Making one's associates feel like valued partners.*
>
> 2) *Responsiveness: Responding to the needs of a partner's customers.*
>
> 3) *Proactive Service: Anticipating needs before they even become apparent.*[39]

These types of relationships support communication and understanding. When the joint focus is on the outcome, people can explore opportunities and expectations that give rise to new solutions.

This kind of real partnership spontaneously erupts from relationships. Among friends, we anticipate needs. For friends, we are willing to work through lunch, bail them out when they haven't adequately planned, and experience a sense of satisfaction from their success.

In the absence of strong relationships, we see posters like the following:

> *Poor planning on your part does not constitute an emergency on my part.*

Take a look at another shining example:

> *The LA office is clueless if it thinks this order is going to get shipped on Friday. I just got the paperwork, and I'm not about to stop everything we've got going just to respond to their little "emergency." They can just forget it.*

The us-versus-them mentality never produces solutions—it just reinforces the problem.

When our relationships are positive and supportive, the entire scenario changes.

People no longer feel like pawns. The switch from a service model to a partnership model makes them the owners in the process. Instead of demanding compliance, offer people a seat at the table; when the dynamics change, individuals thrive, innovation occurs, and results increase.

✦ ✦ ✦

BOP THE GOPHER
LEADERSHIP'S ROLE IN ELIMINATING BAD MANAGEMENT.

Poor management is often like Bop the Gopher.

Most parents have experienced this game at a Chuck E. Cheese's arcade, in which gophers pop up randomly from holes, and the child bops the gopher back into the hole by hitting it with a rubber mallet.

When associates raise issues beyond their pay grade or the confines of their role, bad managers don't see this as an opportunity to engage or grow talent, but quickly move to make sure the person knows his or her place. *Bop!*

Instead, the person's initiative should be honored as a sign of his or her engagement and commitment to the business of the organization. Organizations are starving for leadership, inspiration, creativity, innovation, and engagement. When it pops up, feed it, don't bop it!

Many organizations profess to be places where talent is encouraged to flourish, and yet they restrict contributions, focusing more on *roles.* Capable associates suffer when they experience these limitations.

To be held back by circumstances of birth (gender, race, and physicality) has long offended sensible humans, and

---

AS THE ORGANIZATION TURNS...

The world wide web has created a forum to air the dysfunctional lockstep of bureaucracies. One of our personal favorites is Glassdoor.com, where you can go to revel in the gossip about a wide range of organizations (both distinguished and not).

Our analysis of this site (not scientific, but insightful) revealed approximately 1 laudatory comment to 20 disparaging ones.

It's probably a bit startling as a leader to see your deepest darkest secrets revealed there! Who knew?

✦

such organizations' indiscriminate misuse of talent should fall into the same category and cause equal offense.

High-performance cultures honor contribution above all else, regardless of the level of the individual. When we hear organizations offering a meritocracy, the expectations rise and with it our own chagrin when daily practices make a mockery of those expectations.

> *Research with high performance cultures indicates that confidence in leadership, while a MacroCulture issue, is dramatically affected by the state of the MicroCulture. Approximately half the variance (.49) in employee confidence in leadership can be attributed to the health of the MicroCultures to which they belong.*[40]

Leadership must insure the efficacy of managers for two non-negotiable reasons: 1) to preserve energy that may be "wasted" in in the MicroCulture and 2) because employee's very confidence in leadership is mitigated there.

How do leaders get rid of managers? How do they select and mentor managers to emphasize human talent and capability? Leadership has the ultimate obligation to create paths of growth, innovation, and inspiration by removing the artificial barriers to the use of people's talent, passion, and ability at work.

+   +   +

PEELING AWAY THE ORGANIZATIONAL VENEER

Is it real or is it veneer? In our college days, our furniture would have been lucky to be called veneer, but now we have to look twice at our hardwood floors to know the difference. It seems like everybody is trying to imitate Mother Nature.

In *The Invention of Lying*, Ricky Gervais takes us on a journey through a world where people always say exactly what they mean:

> *I could never marry you because I don't want little fat kids with snub noses.*

> *I loathed every minute I worked for you.*

> *Your baby is so ugly, it's like a little rat.*[41]

When Gervais's character, Mark Bellison, discovers lying, you can almost feel him inventing *organizational veneer*.

Organizational veneer is easier to spot than Marmoleum flooring. It's the smooth epoxy coating over this promise: *We trust our people and see them as our most precious resource.*

Sounds great, but it's important to look closer to discover the truth. Ask these questions:

> *If we really are a precious resource, why is no one listening?*
>
> *Where is the authority to make decisions?*
>
> *What exactly are we trusted with?*

Veneer is hard and smooth, seemingly resistant to damage; however, in actuality, it's usually only one-sixteenth of an inch deep.

Most organizational communication is a type of bureaucratic veneer.

Half a dozen people review the memo until the final version is sufficiently sanitized to send. In the meantime, the entire organization has already heard and digested the news. The only thing left to be determined is the extent to which the official memo matches the truth as we know it.

In the corporate arena, staff chronically prepare leadership with greater zeal and attention to detail than they give to the initiative itself. Perfecting reports more closely resembles sanitizing. Sometimes we refer to this process as You Can't Handle the Truth.[42]

> *How many coats of polish are required before the exec team reviews operational reports or feedback from customers or employees?*

What is the leader to do? Insist on the unadulterated view from those the leader leads and from those they lead.

> *Can you just send me a draft on that? Not polished please, just note your issues and send it on to me.*

Getting fixated on form over function means the Ts are crossed and the Is are dotted, but the candor often disappears with the typos. Reading the plain truth in a timely way is worth a run-on sentence and a dangling preposition.

While there are legitimate, compelling reasons for careful communications, there is really no good reason to varnish the truth. The more authentic the communication, the less disconnect with the MicroCulture.

REAL TRUMPS PRETEND
SPARE US THE FLAVOR OF THE MONTH.

The single most disheartening aspect of organizational life is the struggle to sustain momentum relative to purported goals. How many initiatives fall short of their potential because the follow-through can't stand up to the culture?

Please spare us the program-happy culture and the current flavor of the month.

It is clearly human nature to legitimize our goals by defining programs around them. Imagine an organization without a quality program or an engagement program or a succession-planning program. Would there be any quality, engagement, or upward mobility happening at all?
You might be surprised.

The standard organizational practice is to use programs as a way of institutionalizing desirable behavior or focus within a culture that is either lacking those qualities or is in short supply. Programs are the structural supports of leadership's prescription for change.

Yet programs rarely help continuity, they just provide a language to express where organizations wish it would be.

Quality programs define our interest in having our associates produce defect-free goods and services.

Customer service programs define our interest in seeing our customers have service—or at least the façade of service.

Leadership succession-planning programs define our interest in having our associates become better leaders to succeed the current crop.

We have diversity programs, recycling programs, and WeightWatchers™ programs. Sometimes programs can be associated with increased activity and sometimes with improvement in the scores that measure those activities. Not all of them are bad; some are actually helpful, and a few are outstanding.

This program approach rarely institutionalizes the change it seeks to introduce. The mere act of naming it isolates it from the existing culture.

Program-happy cultures are the antithesis of authentic cultures; however, until recently nobody could identify a more sustainable alternative. How do you continuously evolve your culture?

Moving from an *event mentality* to *connecting mentality* is an important first step. Organizations traditionally undertake engagement and satisfaction measurement on a periodic basis to determine their progress and simultaneously establish commitment to the goal. But the very process of measurement has turned engagement into a survey-related event.

It doesn't make sense to make engagement something we encapsulate and give lip service to once a year.

Developing culture requires year-round, all-encompassing concern that must be integrated into the business of the business. Not as a distinct line item, but rather as the way in which you continuously develop your capabilities to grow.

This is not unlike manager development. While there are programs, classes, discussions, and books to educate and develop managers, the best development is always real-time and comes from real-life experience. For one thing, managers are not always *natural learners*, and for another, they have a job to do and that job is essential to organizational sustainability. Thus, we can't afford to treat their development as a *nice-but-not-essential* aspect of our daily organizational life.

There is little evidence that our manager development programs actually work. Are the manager's capabilities actually produced by the programs or did they previously exist?[43]

The work itself is an enormous, but underutilized, developmental opportunity. Here are the questions we posed to organizations struggling with these issues:

> *Why not coach managers in the business of the business?*
>
> *Why not strengthen your culture in the daily business of the business?*
>
> *Why not highlight associate talents as they enchant your customers?*

Admittedly, the prospect of real-time/real-life development can be scary when practiced on a live customer, but the finest teaching hospitals seem to have mastered it. How much scarier can it be? After all, we practice teaching on live students, we practice cooking on live customers, and we practice comedy on live audiences. And in each case, like a high-wire act, the real deal trumps the pretend in taking the lessons to heart.

Some things simply must be learned in the field.

There is something beautiful about active learning. Opening the process to all the participants at once invites ownership and new thinking. Active learning is least like a *parent-to-child* interaction, more closely resembling a *partner-to-partner, friend-to-friend,* or *colleague-to-colleague* interaction.

+ + +

THAT'S WHY WE CALL IT WORK

We are constantly asking questions to develop a greater understanding of why people do the things they do. One of our personal favorites:

Should work be fun?

The majority of people respond in the same way: "No, that's why they call it *work.*"

This response tells us something about both their experience and their perspective; we're always disappointed to hear it.

Moments of peak performance at work can actually be fun. Ask the salesperson who just closed a mega client after six months of hard pursuit. Ask the teacher who has just taught a second-grader to write. Ask the representative who has helped a customer figure out how to text his granddaughter.

Sadly, there are individuals whose particular role is fraught with problems and troubles, and there are moments of despair when they can't be helped no matter how hard we try (see: the people who issue parking violations). But in those very critical roles and places, there's still joy to be had through the perfect expression of one's talents at work.

If there's no joy in your work, then you aren't doing it right.

Truth be told, some organizations/managers/leaders have a way of sucking the joy right out of the job.

If you've ever had a day that seemed to diminish your soul, you've probably experienced this.

If you've had a manager that seemed to find nothing right about you or your work, you've probably experienced this.

The fitness expert Tony Horton is known for helping people transform their weak and flabby bellies into six-pack abs in an absurdly short period of time. On the infomercial, he credits the notion of muscle confusion for that success.

*Once our muscles become used to an activity, it take less effort
to perform the activity; that means that our results level off—we
"plateau." Breaking the routine means confusing the muscles so that
they have to work harder, and that delivers the best developmental
results.*[44]

Here's our version:

You have to work at work to make work fun.

Consider professional golf. While the pro makes it look easy, the process
itself reflects long, hard, consistent work. Get up, run three miles, hit five
hundred balls, play nine holes, hit five hundred balls, play another nine
holes, resistance train, then hit five hundred more balls.

*A bystander watched Ben Hogan on the driving range hitting balls to
his caddy. He would motion the caddy forward and back several feet. A
few minutes later the observer asked, "Mr. Hogan, it would appear that
you're practicing hitting the ball 175 yards, is that right?"*

*Hogan's response: "No. Actually, I am practicing hitting the ball 174
yards, and I am practicing hitting the ball 176 yards."*[45]

A truly spectacular talent breaks into the spotlight; it sometimes seems
instantaneous. However, upon examination, you will find the person has
continually worked to perfect that talent long before the limelight. Here's
an example from a highly respected consultant:

*"Frank and I recruited hard together, visiting hotels all over the
East Coast. And each day, when we'd finished our last interview, we
continued to talk about talent and opportunity well into the nights and
weekends.*

*Frank was insatiable when speaking about talent within his
organization. We'd spend hours discussing the players, highlighting
the nuances of their talents, identifying the supporting players
and resources they would need, and working to create the right
opportunities to bring the talent along.*

*Those fourteen-hour days were some of the greatest of my career.
We were immersed in great talent. There is nothing more intriguing
than human potential, but seeing the results is what truly brought
everything into focus."*

Working at the work enriches both consultant and CEO and can bring the organization unprecedented growth and success. In Frank's case, the talent within the organization grew alongside the business, and the culture had a certain hum you could see and hear each time you walked into the organization.

Talent can only develop in the face of challenge, and opportunities are necessary for us to stretch and grow. The organizational lesson in muscle confusion is *mix it up,* because predictable is boring, and boring is an unlikely impetus for innovation.

+   +   +

WORRYING ISN'T ENOUGH
GETTING DIRTY IS REQUIRED.

One leader we know liked to preface his frequent about-faces in strategy with this phrase:

> *"We're betting the entire company on this one..."*

This prompted a good many eye rolls from those assembled as they prepared for another leadership-mandated course correction. Sometimes change efforts cannibalize the very things they are trying to produce.

Substantive change takes time and persistence. It often resembles the gentle wave repetitively lapping at the rock, over minutes, months, and years. And like nature, leaders must be persistent, but the energy for the change must come from everyone.

Leaders must be relentless about culture because it represents the total sum of energy available to turn strategy and vision into results. The relentlessness is the key, because the leader's focus is magnified throughout the organization.

It would be nice if we could define three steps and then act accordingly to complete those steps, but culture is too complex and slippery to corral in that way. A great leader is a steward of the organization's culture, but not its dictator or designer.

Leaders must take an active role in "worrying culture along."[46]

Sleepless nights are not required, but consciousness of the issue is all-important.

One of the highest priority concerns should be the quality of the management team. Leadership's rigorous attention to managers will insure the health of the MicroCultures and the connectivity of the bridge. Leaders' actions must match their expectations. They set the standard for excellence with their *own* direct reports, being interested in each person's growth and success. They must act swiftly to improve or remove poor managers. And so on down the line.

Cultures tend to keep doing what they've been doing, so leaders must challenge the status quo in all things structural: policies, processes, and programs. Do they deliver what is needed? The leader's touchpoints offer enormous opportunities to encourage excellence, remove barriers, and highlight line-of-sight. These moments are tangible proof of leadership focus and commitment.

It's the leader's ongoing connection to the culture that enables him to cultivate its virtues. In the next section, we'll explore practical ways for leaders to fuse their interest in culture into their day-to-day business of leadership.

+ + +

Section Five
WHAT TO DO ABOUT IT: CREATING COMPETITIVE ADVANTAGE ACTIVATING OVER ASSESSING

From aspirations to results. How do we make the leap?

Only 14% of all goals achieve the desired results.

Strategy is the rational answer, the grand design, but it is human passion that supplies the momentum to deliver on the goal.

Research suggests only 14% of our goals, initiatives and plans fully achieve success.[47]

When leaders and managers hear this statistic, there is always sharp reaction and disbelief. Yet, as it sinks in, the next question is always, "what is ours?" This is the critical point between assessing and activating. Many would be tempted to institute a measurement program to track all goals and related accomplishments. Makes sense, as we know measurement improves performance, and if you can't measure it, you can't manage it – right?

Let's be clear. This is not a time for measurement, it's a time to focus on activation – the reason the 14 percent are successful! As the illustration above points out, technique, analysis and form are all secondary to the energy needed to produce results. Our focus must be about accelerating the momentum within our culture to realize our goals. What if the percent of success increased from 14 percent to 20, 30, 35 or even 50 percent? How would that impact the success of the business, work team and individual?

First Break All the Rules, introduced some startling discoveries about the distinctions between outstanding and average, discrepancies that accounted for the striking differences in performance between our best (managers and work units) and the rest. That work yielded more than a decade of engagement interventions stimulated by the habits of great managers.

Organizations adopted these "best practices" in their engagement surveys. The items asked were related to business outcomes and reports were provided to the managers of local work units. Managers were encouraged to hold team discussions and required to create action plans to improve results. Today, these methods are in widespread use around the globe, in nearly every organization of appreciable size.

Unfortunately, these tactics are no longer a differentiator of great culture. They are now more reflective of the status quo. Not bad, but timeworn.

Much of the progress made has been in the survey process, but the survey itself while necessary, is simply not sufficient to provide the acceleration needed to inspire great leaps in performance. A survey doesn't create engagement, it just reports on it. And the process itself may be part of the problem.

In spite of the huge rise in knowledge workers, our survey approaches still carry a subtle "parental" message that brings out the "victim" in our employees.

Anonymity often compounds the problem. We promise it because we think our people will feel "at risk" if they provide information that we don't like. Isn't that the definition of a poor culture – a "no-trust" and "kill-the-messenger" kind of culture?

> *Contrast that with organizations where people are provided the option to sign their surveys. The expectation is candid feedback between trusted adults and partners.*

And get this – the information we are seeking to *feedback* came from the people we are going to feed it back to!

Are we saying the survey process is obsolete? Hell yes. More to the point, we are saying it doesn't match the goals we want to achieve.

We want high performance, raving fans and passionate people. You can't get those 3 outcomes from a survey, no matter how convenient the on-line system might be.

In golf, It is the momentum of the club that delivers the impact; everything the golfer does, some 200+ things from grip, feet, head, back, pelvis and shoulders is done to produce the torque required to drive the ball. Most of us with some degree of hand-eye coordination can hit the ball, but the best-in-class, Tiger Woods, Phil Mickelson, Rory McIlroy, etc., define what greatness really is.

McIlroy's dynamic swing generates a ball speed of 176 mph off the club head! There is a bit of "funkiness" to his swing that makes it nearly impossible to duplicate, but the energy produced by it accounts for why he is one of the longest hitters in the game.[48]

In mastering the drive off the tee, the 200+ little things are all important, but the goal is moving the ball down the fairway and that takes energy focused on the ball. If you stop the swing at the top, you destroy the power of its momentum, and your ability to drive the ball.

That's what the typical survey process does — it artificially stops the energy at the worst possible moment, interrupting the momentum of the follow through. We can execute it perfectly, but lose all power in the process.

Let's say for the sake of argument that we had people really excited about taking the survey itself. At that moment, they felt as if their opinion counted and that we were making a concerted effort to listen and incorporate their ideas.

What happens to that energy after the "time out" of one to two months while we compile the data and craft leadership's communication about the results?

After weeks of survey-focused energy, only a tiny fraction of time is invested with our people in a meaningful conversation about them and their work, priorities and goals. Then everyone goes back to their day job until next year.

Do your people actually need a "scorecard" to talk about what really matters at work?

Your objective is to create positive, productive energy that engages the hearts and minds of your people to achieve your business goals. Shouldn't you be talking about that?

Surveys are an adjunct to, not a natural part of, the workplace. No matter how well-executed, surveys introduce an artificial element to conversations about working together that are usually separate from our true goals and priorities. These conversations need to be "acculturated" into everyday working life - creating high performance culture "patterns."

This isn't Nirvana, but it is 2013.   Nothing takes 2 months anymore. Two minutes, two hours or two days, but that's just about the limit of our patience for information.

If your goal is truly to create high performance culture, you need more than assessment.

Our research has concluded that about 80 percent of culture is the same from one organization to another. Every one wants the "CHAIR" (customer focus, honesty, accountability, integrity and respect).   These are not the differentiators; they are the foundations upon which to build.

What differentiates great organizations is their ability to accelerate their momentum toward their results. They ignite an essential spark in their culture - in their people - that generates a relentless pursuit of excellence. It is a unique spark, specific to their cause that excites energy and leads to greatness. It's the 20 percent of culture that yields their distinct competitive advantage - the fervor it takes to deliver amazing results.

There's no Band-Aid for a listless culture.

Culture is too complex to be fit into a box. High performance culture depends upon the organization's unique mission, goals, and results. The one-size-fits-all model doesn't apply.

As we've seen, the assessment process itself may be one of the fundamental barriers in developing more effective cultures. Culture assessment usually becomes an event, a hot topic, but this doesn't necessarily bring about the results organizations are after, because after the initial "diagnosis" there's little momentum left for change.

The CEO of one of the top insurance companies once told us that he wished that there were a saliva test to determine how engaged each person is.

Great point, but little did he know that there is one that already exists.

Ask the person.

We have all been dis-engaged and engaged in our jobs and we knew it. Aside from just being a reliable test, it opens up incredible opportunity for dialogue about a real issue.

That is where engagement is born.

It is much more important to affect culture than to analyze it.
Organizations must become more focused on activation than assessment, and on action rather than analysis.

The approach must reflect a relentless interest in your people's experience, perspective, and yearnings. It is not something to be checked off once a year, but a way of accentuating the energy and enthusiasm of people and keeping them aligned to the purpose all year long.

We communicate our interest in people's views and perspectives through the questions we ask; what we ask sensitizes the organization to what we value.

> *A parade of submarine movies (Hunt for Red October, U-571, Crimson Tide, and Down Periscope) have us thinking about sonar systems, both active and passive. The passive system picks up the sounds around it, allowing the vessel to "run silent, run deep." In contrast, active sonar systems emit a pulse of sound energy that "pings" off its surroundings; the bounce-back, or echo, reveals the nearby objects, but also exposes the submarine in the process.*
>
> *Our questions reveal our interests—just like the sonar pings—and what bounces back gives us insight regarding the de facto culture experienced by our people. We don't know what a culture really is until it is reflected back by the people within.*

Actively pinging leads to many of the outcomes organizations are most interested in producing. A persistent and authentic interest in your people's ideas cultivates the most valuable dynamics: relationship, involvement, ownership, engagement, critical thinking, innovation, and growth. You have nothing to fear by actively pinging because you need your people to know exactly where you stand with respect to the shared culture.

✦   ✦   ✦

THE ANSWER TO ANALYSIS PARALYSIS:
TAKING ACTION.

Many organizations are more focused on conducting research than in the follow-through. It is not uncommon to see leaders turn to focus groups upon receipt of their engagement survey results. We call this dynamic "research about the research." Then, based on the results from the focus groups, these leaders begin to plan some action, which takes place at the macro level. After the plan is set, the leaders communicate the plans throughout the organization.

Having two-plus years of employee research relative to engagement, satisfaction, and confidence, the executive team elected to continue the process with focus groups to probe the employees' point of view.

Their move added months to the timeline before local-level data would be discussed with the people who provided the feedback: the employees. This delay, from the leadership perspective, was warranted because the scores were disappointing and the causes unknown.

On the surface, this appears to be a legitimate endeavor. It has the advantage of opening dialogue with at least some associates and carries the promise of greater understanding. Unfortunately, focus groups affect a minimal number of associates (usually less than 1 percent) and are orchestrated either by leadership or outside consultants, not the line managers or direct supervisors.

Analysis paralysis sends the wrong message about what organizations value. Cultures that study problems more than act are risk-adverse, and progress is reduced to a crawl.

One of our business partners perpetually complains about the newest version of PowerPoint. He says PowerPoint 2003 was "completely ruined" by the so-called improvements in the 2007 version, and now the 2010 version! Don't get him started...

Whenever he begins, I'm tempted to roll my eyes like my teenage daughter, but then I am reminded of a recurring rant of my own. I complain about people's completely irrational resistance to change.

"I don't understand it...I love change. Change is life! It brings opportunity, improvements, new learning..."

My diatribe was recently interrupted by my husband's typically biting wit. "Ah, not so fast, my dear. It's your change you love. The change you are driving. As for everyone else's, you're not so crazy about that either!"

That's right, of course; the control of the change makes all the difference.

There is no benefit in defending or even discussing the merits of change. We evolve or we die. It's a simple proposition, and we pick life every time. But there's pain and fear through the entire journey because we can't control the process and the future is unknown.

Our research points to some very clear human corollaries to change:

1) Control is everything. If you are driving the change, you don't experience the same amount of drama as your customers and associates.
2) During times of change, people focus more on what they have to lose rather than what they have to gain.
3) No matter how long or carefully leaders "craft the message," the people always know what's really going on before they are officially informed.

When leadership hits the pause button until they have everything figured out, everyone is forced to wait. But with the notable exception of wine and cheese, little actually waits well in real life. Produce gets old, people get frustrated, and engagement leaks out as people begin to feel defenseless against the problems or concerns originally identified.

By the time leadership figured it out...we were already in dire straits.

Employees, managers, and customers always reveal that they "knew it first"—long before the research data is analyzed and officially acted upon. In banking, tellers see less and less of their customers until they vanish. In restaurants, wait-staff see the disappointment of regulars in the new menu choices. And technicians see the frustration of dealing with technology that doesn't meet buyer expectations and needs.

Thomas Paine said it best: *"Lead, follow, or get out of the way."*

High-performance cultures are cultures of action. They encourage human initiative and know that understanding comes over time with both action and discovery. The sequence that comes to mind is: Action prompts discovery, which generates new action, which leads to new discoveries, which leads to better action, and then more discovery, etc. And most importantly, everyone on our teams can play that game, together, at all levels of the organization.

Where we start doesn't matter; it's where we end up that counts.

Not to be facetious, but it really doesn't matter where leaders start when deliberately developing their organization's culture. The culture already exists and it's already evolving, so if you love the results you are getting, then there's no rush. But for many leaders, the gap between what they want and what they are getting is cause for angst.

The strategy gap is not static, but is highly time-sensitive. Results are always subject to the reality of diminishing returns: what might have constituted a huge win a year ago may only take us to average today. As the pace of change increases it pays to be the best <u>and</u> the fastest to the goal line.

As radical as it may sound, we propose to *just start*. The beginning must be accompanied with an unwavering commitment to persist and an openness to take the action and discovery wherever it leads and to whomever it concerns. Unlike most organizational initiatives, this one has a beginning but not an end, as it reflects a way of thinking and working with people that will lead to a great culture.

If something goes awry, you have tomorrow. As long as you keep going, you can fix almost anything.

+   +   +

A PRACTICAL APPROACH
FOR EVOLVING CULTURE INTO A COMPETITIVE ADVANTAGE.

Cultural Connection is an inquiry-based approach that deliberately "pings" the aspects of the culture you wish to enhance or revitalize. By pinging, you fortify the strengths of your culture in the process of understanding it.

Cultural Connection is an organizational sonar system that activates culture via three interrelated disciplines:

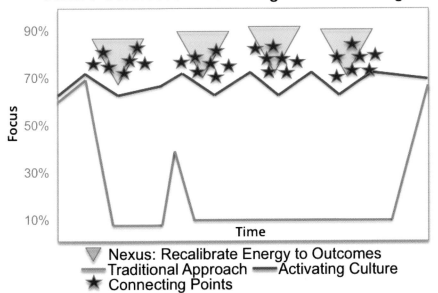

1) **Connecting Points:** A day-to-day attentiveness and interest in the culture;
2) **Nexus Points:** A deliberate and focused action on the intersection between culture and business; and
3) **Cultural P&L**: A year-to-date view of cultural gains.

+ + +

CONNECTING POINTS
PRACTICING DAY-TO-DAY ATTENTIVENESS.

Because culture is built moment-by-moment in the touchpoints between people (associates, managers, and leaders), its effectiveness can only be understood from the perspective of the people participating.

Using touchpoints as an opportunity to ask about how things are working is an elegant way of showing interest. This creates a cultural connecting point. The topics of connecting points could range from feedback about policies and practices to insight about strategies and line-of-sight to the customer.

While a single leader cannot drive everything he or she wants to see within the organization, the leader's interest accelerates progress.

Tom was a talented CEO at a large agency with a huge concern: He was a great coach and consultant to his fifty salespeople, but he simply couldn't keep up.

In consultation with Tom, we discovered that he was spending the majority of his time with his low performers. No matter how long he worked with them, they needed more. On the other hand, his top performers were all capable of running their own businesses, and while he admired and depended upon them, he rarely spent much face time with them.

We urged Tom to focus on his best players—and to make clear to the sales organization that his best performers had earned his time and attention. Tom was doubtful—but agreed to the proposition.

Months later, the biggest discovery was Tom's. He learned that he had been out of touch with his best sellers' techniques; he confessed to learning more from them than perhaps they had from him. He also found that his middle performers stepped up their game, since he had made it explicit that by doing so they would benefit from his attention and support. Even some of his lower performers increased beyond his

*expectations when he changed his investment of time, because they
missed his support and increased their performance to get it back.*

Tom had inadvertently been sending the message that the people who
needed him most would get his attention. In some ways, he had been
accentuating the needy over the successful—and got more needy
employees in the process!

When Tom began to focus on excellence, his touchpoints with his people
brought out what he really valued: results. Moments like these are
opportunities to stimulate the kind of culture that produces innovation and
exemplary performance.

When the pinging goes viral...

For a culture to yield the kind of competitive advantage the organization
needs to "beat the crap out of the competition" (as a great CEO once
gingerly stated), then it has to be a unified effort. Associates aren't just
dependents within the cultural landscape, but determinants of it. They
must take their rightful role as full partners in the development of the
culture, as well as the business.

The advantages are exponential when our associates pick up the mandate
by becoming more interested in their service partners' needs. When
this happens, the pinging goes viral and everyone benefits from the
increased energy that comes from better understanding, relationships, and
commitment.

Taking time to inquire into the culture is a leader/manager/associate
obligation in the same way that the entire team shares the obligation to
produce results.

Targeted pinging is a navigational must.

In the last decade, there has been a definitive trend in the data relative
to culture.   The populations (organizationally and nationally) have been
effectively "pulling apart," becoming more polarized, with fewer people
straddling the middle.

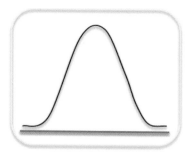

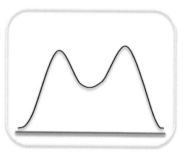

Figure 1 represents the more traditional distribution (bell curve) of attitudes, where the majority of people are in the middle.

Figure 2 represents a bi-modal distribution, where people are split on opposite sides of the continuum.

People are taking a more dichotomous view than ever before; with our latest research indicating only about 23 percent of people are "passengers" within our organizations. This number is down 17 percent from only 3 years ago, and reflects a tendency for people to either be very engaged at work (actively engaged) or actively dis-engaged.

	Actively Engaged	Passengers	Actively Dis-engaged
2010	31%	40%	29%
2013	43%	23%	35%

Practically speaking, this has huge ramifications for the way in which we lead and manage organizations. Faced with organizational course corrections, we will increasingly see people responding with either full enthusiasm or deep despair, with a few undecided.

The most dramatic consequence of this movement will be to our practice of leading by consensus. A polarized culture is not likely to achieve consensus anytime soon, so the longer it takes leadership to accept this, the more time and momentum will be lost.

In the past, our research with top performers has consistently highlighted their greater contribution to organizational performance. But in light of the polarization of our cultures, their impact is even more critical; top performers must now be seen as key activators of great culture.

People are the culture, but top performers are the key to cultural greatness. When creating high-performance cultures, we must systematically ping our best—our top producers. As Tom discovered, their achievements, commitment, and line-of-sight to the customers make their insight invaluable to the organization.

Ask about their goals and needs. Find out what works and what does not. Which customer challenges demand innovation? The more insight you gather from top performers, the more clearly you'll understand the path to excellence.

Within that group of top performers, we must identify the "early adopters." They are instrumental to our agility and responsiveness; as cultural change agents, they are invaluable.

This is not to suggest that we ignore the needs of any group, but leaders need to systematically focus more on those who can help create and sustain the movement. Passengers will follow.

+   +   +

NEXUS POINTS THE INTERSECTION OF BUSINESS AND CULTURE.

High performance culture is not a separate concern, it is how we can achieve and sustain our competitive advantage. This is the real reason we must connect our culture with the business of our business.

Cultural improvement, applied like a "program" commands attention like an event in the stream of organizational life. Yet performance is the result of a complex interaction between the individual's capabilities, organizational expectations and the context (physical and psychological) and it is an ongoing concern.

Our culture research has demonstrated that productive energy – the energy available to deliver organizational results – is a product of the psychological connection in the MicroCulture. Moment to moment, this energy varies based on the vitality of the individual's connection to the team, manager, and purpose of work.

Engagement is not enough; we need to engage our people in the achievement of our most critical business imperatives associated with their roles and teams.

> Engagement in the hypothetical - that is, a traditional survey and feedback process - doesn't always help us to achieve our desired business results. We might "feel more engaged" but to really impact

business results we need to engage our hearts and minds around the purpose and meaning of our work.

What we need is to engage our people in the business of the business – not once a year or twice a year, but in a way that builds the connection, understanding, and performance between managers and team members and bridges between departments.

Imagine that today; Jane (team member) and Jim (manager) have a productive conversation about the three most critical performance outcomes for the next three months. Jane identifies several aspirational goals for herself and steps she will take to achieve them. The conversation is strengths focused, so it encourages Jane to identify the people who she needs to support her, and perhaps the infrastructure elements she needs most to assure success.

The conversation allows a closer alignment between Jane and Jim, and an increased awareness of Jane's view of her situation and goals as well as Jim's perspective and counsel. It's a worthy start.

Great managers do this in a very natural way that helps them increase per person productivity on their teams. Other managers may not be as intentional or as effective at the process.

A week or two passes during which Jane identifies some early success. Minutes later, Jim reviews it and recognizes the gains made; he takes the opportunity to suggest that Jane pull a colleague from Marketing into her plans, as she is already ahead of schedule.

Excellence is about "multiplying" rather than dividing. It is the manager's role to accelerate performance, not "correct it."

Three weeks pass; Jim's manager, Carl, who has been following the pace of achievement across several departments, takes the opportunity to recognize Jim's success as a connector – a bridge between departments: three of his team members are ahead of plan on results, and connected to organizational partners. This connection resulted in the identification of 2 system changes that would simplify a joint process and eliminate several time-consuming steps.

What began as Jane's business imperative, and Jim's suggestions, now crosses several organizational groups, and is still ahead of schedule and picking up advocates. Jim's suggestion and Jane's activation of those suggestions crossed organizational boundaries and improved relationships, process and overall productivity.

Managers are catalysts within the bridge culture; their role is to connect people to purpose, removing barriers and providing opportunities for better leverage. Just as "failed connections" build mistrust and drain energy, relationships build a willingness to anticipate the needs of our new partners.

We are after higher performance. But often our organizational systems only track "after game stats" – too late to help us improve. The best managers capitalize on people's inherent strengths and literally "catch people doing something right" to optimize the performance curve.

How many latent opportunities are missed in the day-to-day life of an organization, like better efficiencies, new sales and delighting customers? What if you could spot them and license people to use their talent to capitalize on such moments? As relationships among and across our groups increase, so does our potential to spot opportunities for maximizing performance.

In every organization, there exists a set of business factors that are critical to performance improvement. For some, the challenge is sales. For others, better efficiencies or relevant innovation. While the unique nature of the challenge varies (with time and market conditions), business imperatives almost always revolve around (1) sales growth, (2) customer acquisition, (3) customer retention, and (4) innovation and product development.

If culture is to become your competitive advantage, the culture must be aligned to the unique business imperative of the organization. This will close the strategy gap (the gap between desires and results).

The intersection of business and culture creates the nexus point—a sweet spot for improving execution.

Organizations have poor tolerance for the nonessential. Unfortunately, important things are sometimes considered nonessential when they are compared to other more urgent concerns—*fires*. That is precisely why it is so difficult to get traction for cultural change; people can recognize its importance, but not its urgency.

To gain traction and results, cultural concerns must fit the business equation. Getting our people's perspective (rational and emotional) directed to specific challenges is a nexus point that can activate both business and culture.

Unlike the organizational survey, which divides assessment and action, a nexus point is an opportunity for collective collaboration around a key topic of concern. Going back to our sonar example, it would be the equivalent of pinging the organization around a critical cultural or business issue, not to surface data, but to ignite conversations that engage, energize, and inspire action.

Research suggests that the best way to instigate a collective focus is by seeding the culture with questions designed to bring out the best in the culture, engaging the minds and hearts of the people on the topic.

Getting managers and associates talking about relevant issues together is like throwing a pebble into a pool—it ripples throughout the culture.

One organization with long-tenured staff struggled with the challenge of gearing the culture toward individual performance.

Discussions with top performers in this organization revealed their frustration with management's chronic inattention to poor performers. In the face of increased pressure to produce with fewer people, their high-performing managers and associates were unhappy that the nonproductive employees failed to meet their obligations. This prompted leadership to make this business issue a nexus point for the culture.

Leaders and managers committed to the nexus point and continued the conversations started with the organization's top performers. Shouldn't everyone have the benefit of such a conversation? Performance feedback moved from an event to an expectation, connected to the organization's mission and purpose. This enabled managers to systemically communicate that the underlying value system of the culture—its religion—was not changing.

As conversations about performance took place among of its members, the culture began to react. Top performers began to see their feedback taken seriously; they felt understood and valued.

The nexus point is more than discovery—it is action. In the case above, the actions included reviewing both the barriers and enablers within the organization to support the desired change. This meant focused manager/leader development and careful reviews of the processes and procedures around employee performance. The direct focus on individual performance enabled the organization's management/leadership and associates to take action in a way that positively improved their culture as well as their results.

In this case, no single dimension would likely have proven successful or impactful. A culture resists change engineered from the top, but this change started in the grassroots—with the organization's high performers.

The nexus point is a way of engaging your people around a dimension critical to its performance and growth. This isn't about installing a change; it's about inviting members of the organization to share in the discovery and ownership of what should be changed, from their perspective.

In the above example, the organization's commitment to the change was reinforced by a pulse-check with employees. Feedback directly from the staff members confirmed the relevance and impact of the actions managers and leaders were taking. This pulse-check, specifically focused on the nexus point, inspired confidence in leadership and management actions.

To influence the evolution of the culture, the questions asked must reflect what the organization wants to see. Keeping it simple can offer distinct advantages that a full-on employee survey may not.

The best way to focus a culture around a business imperative is to encourage conversation. Getting individual employees directly involved is crucial.

✛   ✛   ✛

CASE STUDY:
THE POWER OF NEXUS IN A HIGHLY SPECIALIZED ENGINEERING FIRM:

A high-performance engineering organization was experiencing record growth. Sales are often the crux of an organization's business concerns, but in this case, sales were robust and growing. The organization's sales channel involved both an architect (client) and their customer, both of whom needed to be delighted with the process and results to insure their retention and future business.

While the sales were forthcoming, the organization struggled with a couple of issues that threatened their growth: (1) the hand-off from business development to service and (2) the variance in their professional staff, the project managers who managed the architect interface and service. These issues were not new, and prior to our involvement, a number of moves were made to correct them. These moves were "best practices" borrowed from other high-performing service organizations, but failed to deliver sustainable impact.

From our vantage point, these two issues, being critical business imperatives, were the ideal nexus for cultural alignment.

With deliberate attention to their top performers, solutions started to emerge, which involved structural, procedural, and human cultural elements. Over the course of several months, the organization was able to undo a few of their cultural misfires and better align their culture to their challenge.

The organization implemented a new hand-off process between business development and service that started each project off on the right foot, minimizing architect/customer distress and confusion.

Taking a cue from their top performer's playbook, the hand-off process was welcomed by both sales and project management teams, as it codified an element of the business that had been cause for frustration. Simple, smart, and effective, it met with approval from the clients and customers and paved the way for the service team to carry the ball on the project.

Culture is how we see ourselves and this organization identified itself as poor in service. Unfortunately, this message was being communicated to clients and customers through the implementation of two customer service policies: a reporting requirement and a customer service call.

The organization eliminated an energy-draining reporting requirement from the project manager's to-do list.

The reporting requirement had been designed to insure that progress on each project was communicated directly to customers. Unfortunately, this reporting requirement used up copious amounts of project management time and resulted in very little information communicated to the architect; most of the reports were simply confirmations that the project was on track.

The organization eliminated a "what mistakes have we made lately" customer service call conducted by an outside vendor.

The customer service call was not a service enhancer. It actually encouraged dissatisfaction when the representative could not answer questions about the actual project; the call became an unfortunate signal to the customer that their project was not top of mind to the service organization. Eliminating the call increased the perception of service.

The organization implemented an "exception" call by project managers to communicate critical information to the client.

The new communication was a purposeful call: a personal call to the client whenever the project slipped from the timeline. This was welcomed as it allowed the client to get involved immediately to help solve the problem and meet the scheduled completion dates. Moreover, since the call was made directly by the project manager, it improved relationships, service, and project timelines

Talent in the project manager role was a critical nexus point for this organization because the project manager was responsible for all aspects of service after the sale. The technical nature of the work required expertise in various industries, and, together with the talent requirements, selection of new project managers was a difficult and often frustrating process. Bringing both elements, talent and expertise, into focus meant that individuals could be more effectively cast into the right role.

Project managers who excelled at the technical aspects of their role but were poor managers were recast into technical practice leader roles.

The new practice leaders were delighted with the changes, which highlighted their individual preferences and strengths. They were relieved from people management, which had frustrated and drained them. Instead, they functioned as the industry experts they truly were, and this took the pressure off the project manager role.

The most talented project managers were used to create a recruiting and selection protocol.

The new talent-focused selection model heightened concerns for talent, but lessened the technical requirements around the project manager role. This increased the organization's ability to add key staff more quickly, keeping pace with the organization's sales goals.

The focus on the nexus enabled the organization to make the changes that mattered most from the vantage point of their top performers, and in record time. The entire process was completed in a few months and with a high degree of commitment, engagement, and enthusiasm on the part of the entire project management teams; their ideas became the framework of the change.

The organization described above had a highly specialized business niche and brand promise. The nexus point focused members on the specifics of their roles, their line-of-sight, and their contributions to the business, and for that reason it improved energy, results, and ownership within.

The best solutions are never generic.

Transporting the exact solution deployed above to another organization, even in the same business service arena, would not likely yield the same results. The efficacy of the nexus point stems from its tight focus on the business of the business.

✦ ✦ ✦

CULTURAL P&L
TURNING A CULTURAL PROFIT.

Financial P&Ls monitor wealth; Cultural P&Ls monitor health. It is always incumbent upon leadership to determine the status quo against its goals and plans for the future. There are a number of ways to do that, and a full-scale employee survey is one of them. However, as we have noted, the employee survey is not the optimal starting point for change; it functions more effectively as an index or reference point of successful movement.

Leaders need a Cultural P&L to assess the relative gain (or loss) in all three levels of culture: Micro, Bridge, and Macro. Within each level, two basic categories of information should be included:

1) the must-have elements of culture, which we have called *cultural cornerstones*, and

2) data unique to your organization's nexus points, based on your goals, brand promise, and strategy.

The following examples are based on cultural cornerstones that every organization's Cultural P&L should include.

MICROCULTURE P&L

The MicroCulture is the foundation of the Cultural P&L; it reflects the raw energy available to the organization. Engagement, the measure of positive and productive energy, is the cultural cornerstone—a necessary first step in cultural revitalization and alignment.

Of particular concern is the quality of energy within the MicroCultures of the organization; Actively Engaged people report using (on average) 82 percent of their capacity at work, while more Actively Dis-Engaged people are using only about 27 percent. Leadership's ability to pinpoint these differences is the first step to managing them.

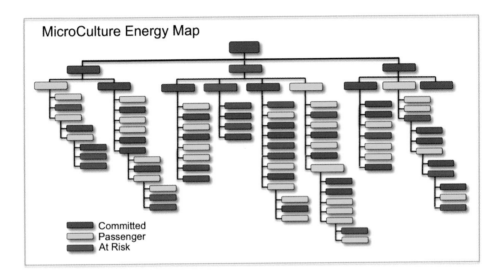

MicroCulture Energy Map

Committed
Passenger
At Risk

Minimally, the MicroCulture component of the P&L would include:

1) An energy map of the organization identifying areas where people are invested, connected, and focused versus areas that are at risk. (The figure above, the MicroCulture Energy Map, shows unit-by-unit differences in energy.)

2) The variance between MicroCultures, reflecting the range in managerial effectiveness.

3) Energy level trends over time indicating gains or loss in raw energy.

The purpose of the MicroCulture P&L is to bring the individual work-unit energy into focus. An effective P&L allows leadership to identify areas of strength, where the energy is purposeful and productive, versus those areas where the organization's energy is diluted or wasted.

BRIDGECULTURE P&L

An effective BridgeCulture is critical to innovation, synergy, and overall performance. Successful bridges enable people to overcome interdepartmental barriers to deliver extraordinary results.

As breakdown, or fractures in the BridgeCulture occur, organizational results suffer; true innovation and process improvement is often unrealized due to such schisms. The energy between groups can be either productive or non-productive, as reflected by the Energy Map depicted in the figure below.

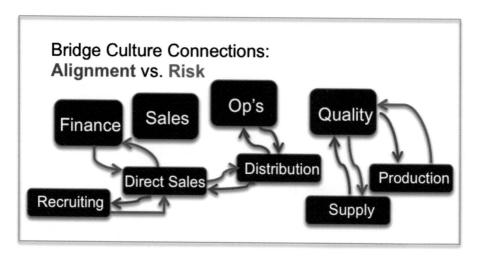

The BridgeCulture component of the P&L should include:

1) An energy map of the interconnections or bridges between key service partners, identifying the relative alignment or risk associated with the connection.
2) A reciprocal view between departments for identifying opportunities for leadership, process, or system improvements and customer impact.
3) Bridge-level trends over time, indicating gains or losses in connectivity.

The purpose of the BridgeCulture P&L is to provide leadership with insight regarding the efficacy of the hand-offs among departments within the organization. The synergy inherent within the organization is dependent upon the quality of the connections between these groups.

+ + +

MACROCULTURE P&L

The MacroCulture cornerstones include broader cultural variables that are important for all organizations, such as belonging and loyalty. The MacroCulture P&L should help leaders to ascertain how well the culture is aligned to the organization's strategy and to determine future priorities. The MacroCulture component of the P&L should include:

1) Confidence in leadership, strategy, and vision and overall satisfaction (with internal and external benchmarks).
2) The trends or stability of the MacroCulture variables, indicating gains or losses.

The purpose of the MacroCulture P&L is to clarify the overall satisfaction levels of members and the degree of confidence in leadership, strategy, and the vision; it captures associate attraction to the overall organization.

+ + +

HOW TO INTEGRATE NEXUS POINTS INTO THE CULTURAL P&L

The Cultural P&L must also include the elements of culture that represent competitive advantage, that is, the alignment to the business imperatives. Of course, these will vary greatly across organizations, as the specific nexus points depend on the real-time challenges facing the organization.

The measurement of nexus points may involve a mix of customer and employee data to link both the promise and the delivery. A great example of this can be found in pharmaceutical and medical sales, where there is a gap between the activities of the company and the actual writing of prescriptions. Typically, representatives are trained in the products, in sales techniques and strategies—that is, best practices. But when competing sales representatives converge in the doctor's waiting room, what constitutes excellence? What drives market share?

In a pharmaceutical/medical device organization we'll call AmMedico, the physician's needs became a critical nexus point. These needs determined (1) which representatives were seen by the doctor and (2) whether or not products were used and recommended as a result.

Research directly with physicians allowed us to identify the cultural elements that contributed most to physician loyalty. These elements clustered into three levels:

(1) Inform Me, (2) Make it Easy for Me, and (3) Make Me Better. While the first two levels were important to physician satisfaction, only the third tier (Make Me Better) represented loyalty—the competitive advantage.

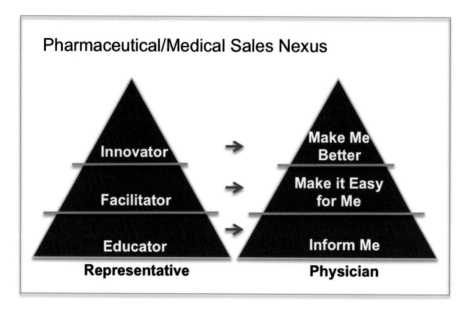

Make Me Better was the sweet spot for market share. The representative's focus on improving the physician's ability to treat his patients and grow his practice was the nexus of competitive advantage for AmMedico.

There are some challenges associated with the measurement of nexus points, but these challenges should be embraced as part and parcel to the process. In the struggle to find the best way to assess what we want, our focus is sharper. Sharing this challenge with our people improves both the measurement and the ultimate results.

As a research organization, we feel compelled to point out that it is both unrealistic and unnecessary to seek out external benchmarks for nexus point data; efforts to do so may cut short the organization's ability to define and precisely measure the cultural elements that deliver their unique brand promise or business imperative. Effective customer loyalty measurement recognizes this inherent disconnect and gets very personal to the organization to deliver relevance. When we seek out standardized measures for what is a unique circumstance, we lose the power of precision and dilute the focus of our people and our process.

+ + +

COLLECTING DATA FOR THE CULTURAL P&L

The organization's Cultural P&L can be accomplished in a number of ways. The most obvious is the traditional survey approach, complete with its unintended consequences.

We advocate another path: activating over assessing.

Our favorite method is to collect "snapshots" of the culture through mini pulse-checks done in conjunction with the nexus points. This method lessens the tendency for the survey process to be treated as an event and increases the real time collaboration and conversation around important cultural issues.

Using the nexus point as a catalyst, it becomes much easier to jump-start conversations about how we work together.

> *When people respond to survey questions, their interest is heightened. What did other people say? What does it mean for me? For my team?*

> *Providing people with individual feedback upon completion of the survey items stimulates this natural interest.*

> *What if we provided associates with a forum to discuss these questions in real time? It is their perception we are really after, isn't it?*

Contrast that scenario with the traditional survey results model:

> *Joe the Manager brings in his report two-plus months after the survey and holds it defensively against his chest. He begins, "According to the data..."*

> *Around the room, glancing surreptitiously, associates are trying to remember the items, their own responses, and meanwhile gauging Joe's mood.*

Only in organizations would we dare to tell people what they feel.

Providing feedback directly to the individual employee acknowledges the real goal of the process, that is, engaging the associate in the important work of improving culture, starting with his or her own strengths and current state of energy.

People want to improve and are hungry for individual feedback and development; responding directly to them is one of the best ways to encourage them to come to the table as owners of the challenge. The energy associated with immediate feedback is a significant advantage over traditional methods that often take months and usually fail to re-engage the team's energy and focus.

Sustaining momentum is easier than creating it; once we get people going, we need to encourage the movement.

When the people are no longer dependent upon the manager to bring data back to the team, the questions cultivate commitment at the individual employee level. Bringing associates and management together in real time to talk about the nexus point and ways to improve the work environment can create collaboration and problem-solving at all levels (Micro-, Bridge-, and MacroCulture).

It isn't necessary for assessment to be a separate initiative; we can track the effectiveness of our culture-in-motion and still provide a meaningful Cultural P&L. Employee energy can be assessed, overall satisfaction and leadership confidence determined, and managerial effectiveness can be monitored. The leadership team can use this data to make both strategic and practical decisions without delaying organizational conversations.

No matter how the Cultural P&L is created (through a traditional process or a more activating approach), leadership must set aside time to review and reflect on the state of culture as a way of identifying new opportunities for development, impact, and improvement. This should happen more than one time each year. The Cultural P&L, built over the quarters of the year, lends itself to this goal and the selection of a critical nexus point for organizational focus. The Cultural P&L is an organic way to manage our most precious resource: the zeal, energy, and focus of our people.

+ + +

ESCAPE FROM THE LAND OF NO
WHERE GREAT IDEAS GO TO DIE.

Recently, in the midst of an executive team discussion, Stan, a talented friend, colleague, and client, quipped:

> *"The Land of No, where great ideas go to die."*
>
> *Instantly, the entire group grasped the significance. The Land of No is a place where passion, innovation, and hope can be trapped by the simplest word in the English language.*
>
> *The Land of Yes is a state less defined but far removed—where possibilities are endless and enthusiasm contagious.*

The Land of Yes is great culture.

We began our journey with a single overriding concern:

> *How do we create a culture that engages the hearts and minds of our people, connects their passion to the organization's purpose, and delivers extraordinary performance?*

In other words, how do we create a culture that fulfills our collective dream for a successful future?

In the decades of work that contributed to this book, thousands of individual interviews, research projects, and surveys revealed the secrets of extraordinary cultures and their uninspiring counterparts—cultures that violate employees' sensibilities and mock their values. Each discovery added to our collective awareness of culture; each piece of the puzzle forced us to reconcile the intent of our actions with the reality of our results.

It has been a bittersweet journey, full of high expectations and scattered with disappointments.

Our discoveries have led to a deeper appreciation of a simple truth: *The core of the culture is the individual.* The very essence of all organizational energy lies in each individual member. Again and again, we are reminded of a profound statement:

> *We have completely undersold the potential of every living human being on the planet.*
>
> *—Dr. James A. Sorensen*

Excellence begins with each individual, capable of amazing creativity, inspiration, and fortitude, with potential for incredible acts of kindness, generosity, and service. An organization must celebrate the variation in human talent, perspective, and capability as the fundamental strength of its culture.

Extraordinary performance begins with the MicroCultures, where each person's individuality connects with his or her role, team, and manager. MicroCultures that honor individuality and create trusting environments bring out the best of each member. This is not an exhaustive proposition, but a simple one:

1) Help me know what is expected of me—and how what I do adds value.
2) Know me, trust me, and accept me as your full partner.
3) Let me use my gifts to contribute, grow, and to realize my own potential as a talented person.

All associates are conduits for a successful Culture Connection. Everyone shares reciprocal responsibilities to accept, to help, to honor, and to inspire the culture to which they belong.

We look to the organizational structure for guidance—the definitions of our jobs/roles, the workflow, and the procedural rules that define our interconnectivity. At each juncture where humans interact with structure, an opportunity is born; the outcome may either be something greater than, or less than, the sum of its parts.

These opportunities belong to the BridgeCulture, which can galvanize individual tribes from departments or create an extended, synergistic community that supports everyone's goals. Managers and leaders are catalysts for bridging these interdepartmental chasms keeping us from our desired results.

The qualities that make an organization excellent are about 80 percent generic (cultural cornerstones) and 20 percent specific (nexus points).

Competitive advantage lies in the 20 percent that slam-dunks the brand promise to the customer, the focused line-of-sight between your people and your customers. It is incumbent upon each organization to identify those business-centric elements of their culture and touch on those topics throughout their cultural inquiry.

Finally, we must create a culture where people can throw off the bonds of "organizational-itude," that victim-like mentality that keeps us coloring within the lines, in favor of line-of-sight-induced passion and individuality that invents a new level of service excellence.

The Land of No is a mentality born in fear and articulated by control. A shift in our fundamental beliefs about people and their capability can elevate our thinking and our future.

To do that, we must reverse the natural order of the hierarchy and engineer a certain degree of chaos amid the organizational design, particularly around the business imperatives of our brand/strategy.

Everyone sees the perils of chaos, but great leaders know that control is a double-edged sword.

To get hearts and minds in the game, we must allow our associates to take the lead in teaching us what our cultures really are and how they affect our results.

The truth is that:

- Energy once expended (purposeful or not) cannot be reclaimed.
- Leadership not followed is hollow position-ship.
- Trust when broken may never be fully restored.

For sure, high-performance culture is not simple—nor is it enduring. Like lightning in a bottle, it can't be stored. Its very nature means that we must be relentlessly interested in it—or face the consequences of our inattentiveness.

In the economic struggles of today, size, history, and track records offer little assurance of success. Our competitors change with the technological landscape, forcing us to adapt to an emerging marketplace we have never seen before.

While virtually nothing stays the same in our marketplaces, we find ourselves pretending that it has as we continue to trust in our conventional human resource systems, our managerial checks and balances, and our quality processes. As leaders, we strive to provide the most compelling vision to our people, a cutting-edge strategy to our marketplace, and new brand promises to our customers. We work tirelessly to get our people on board with our plans in an effort to reliably and consistently deploy them.

And through the very process of doing these things we tend to disenfranchise the people we need the most.

What we really need to "beat the crap out of the competition" goes well beyond the capabilities of top-down leadership.

The future we can't quite imagine will be ushered in on the energy of individuals and the passion of their connection to the customer and the team. Will these individuals thrive within your organization—or will they jump ship to your competitors? Perhaps they will join the thousands of people who in the last decade seceded from traditional organizations to create their own?

Whether or not we like to accept it, the most spectacular breakthroughs have not come from organizations, but from the people within them (or on the fringes). Extraordinary results have always come from the human spark that connects passion to purpose.

The future is waiting to be achieved through the actions we take today. We all have a choice to make:

- As individual employees, we can take our assigned seats as dutiful passengers and hope that our leaders can move us toward a better (or at least palatable) future. Or we can take the risk in acting as owners of the cultures we care about.

- As managers, we can keep working to stabilize the boat while we pass leadership's expectations down and through to our people, controlling the chaos. Or we can become catalysts for inspiration, creativity, and service by encouraging each person's talent and contribution.

- As leaders, we can perfect credible and compelling visions of the future and sell them to our people. Or we can demonstrate a genuine and relentless interest in the power of our people, their insight, and their connection to our customers and brand.

There is risk in the Land of Yes, but the greater risk lies in constraining the talent, inspiration, and passion of our own people.

✦ ✦ ✦

APPENDIX
GETTING STARTED

While each organization is distinct, our research suggests that some areas are particularly helpful for starting a cultural inquiry in your organization. In the following section, we frame these areas and offer a set of questions that leaders have told us they found helpful in queuing up connecting points with their people and in identifying nexus points for aligning their culture with their strategy.

Before beginning, keep these principles in mind:

- Brief, authentic touchpoints are more valuable than long, drawn-out discussions that end up more philosophical than practical. Think of this as a catalyst for fostering relationship, reflection and action, not a decision-making or consensus-building process.

- Be relentlessly interested in your top performers; they have earned the right to your time and they likely have the strongest line-of-sight to your customer. It is a way to engage people in some of the most meaningful and thought-provoking concerns in your business.

- Everyone should be interested in the perspective of team members, partners, managers, and leaders. The same inquiry process can be used by anyone at any time for any issue of concern. It's a spontaneous process of discovery and action, rediscovery and new action. When highly successful, your interest in others will go viral as other leaders, managers, and associates pick up a way of relating to one another, customers, and all relevant challenges.

Connecting Points

In the following section, we provide a two-step process to help provoke conversations with your organization or team:

1) Questions to ask yourself.
2) Questions to ask your top performers.

Use your discoveries to identify nexus points to take the process to the next level. High-performance culture requires commitment to accentuate what you want more of within the culture.

A conversation is like a fire...once started you never know how far it will spread.

STRATEGY

We define the strategy gap as the distance between our goals and our results. While we can't completely rule out the notion that the strategy itself is flawed, most of the time problems stem from the way the strategy is being executed.

Leaders must start with their own assessment of the situation, both in terms of expectations and results.

Ask yourself:

- What elements of your strategy (market/brand) have changed over the past twelve months?
    - How has the organization responded or adjusted to those changes?
    - What aspects of your strategy are currently being executed to excellence (90+ percent)?
    - In what aspects of your strategy is execution lagging behind?
    - What programs/strategies are being provided to support that area?
- Given the timeline and goals that you set, what results have been achieved in relation to those expected?
    - How satisfied are you about the progress to date?
    - If you could, what changes would you make?
- If you did not have a sales problem today, what other problems would you have?
- What are some of the biggest gaps you see between your culture and your strategy?

When executing strategy, the issues sometimes lie in the failure of the MicroCulture to truly understand or agree with it. To probe that issue, your inquiry must extend beyond your own circle to determine how well the organization understands the strategy and the rationale behind it.

Connecting Points: Be interested in how your people see the strategy of the organization—its clarity, appropriateness, and how well it is currently being executed.

Ask top performers:

- Now that it has been in place for a time, how do you see the strategy working?
    - What aspects are working well?
    - What aspects are we struggling with?
- What results have you seen (from your team, customers, divisions, etc.)?
- How confident are people (you) in the strategy? How are they (you) feeling about it?

VISION

The vision is rarely as clear as leadership imagines. Frequently, the variation of vision and mission within the leadership team is significant. This results in a suspended belief in the organization's official version of the story.

Ask yourself:

- To describe your vision for your organization.
- What are the most critical elements of your value proposition to your customers?
    - In your opinion, what differentiates you from your competitors?
- Thinking about the growth and value of your organization overall, what would you say are your strengths?
    - Thinking about the growth and value of your organization overall, what would you say have been your limitations or barriers?
- What are the core values of the organization?
    - Of those core values, which do you feel are the ones that "stir" people the most?
- What inspires you about your organization?

Because meanings are in the people and not the message, you must know how the vision is being interpreted by associates. Is it relevant to their role? Is it relevant to their contribution?

Connecting Points: Be interested in your people's vision or view of the organization and the relationship they see with the customer. Be curious about what inspires them.

Ask top performers:

- What is your vision of our organization?
- What do you see as the most critical aspects of our value proposition (or value promise) to the customer?
- What are the best aspects of our culture?
- What are the values you see in evidence every day?
- What inspires you about your role in relation to our customers?

CULTURE

When the distinction between science and religion is blurred within the culture, its members tend to fight change regardless of its intention. In the most successful cultures, the science must set a pace beyond that of competitors while holding onto the religion of the organization, the line-of-sight to the customer.

Ask yourself:

- What are the most salient aspects of your organization's culture? (What words come to mind to describe it?)
  - How do these attributes compare to the most effective organizations (or cultures)?

Distinguish science (always evolving) from religion (static and entrenched). Preserve the core values of the organization while continually refining how those values are celebrated and lived out every day. Hunt down hypocrisy, which saps the energy of the organization (and the confidence of everyone in it), and replace it with your personal commitment. Write your name on those values.

- What aspects of your culture are evolving (changing the most)?
- What aspects of your culture are resolute (unchanging, deeply held)?
  - What traditions characterize the organization?
  - What do they (the traditions) imply we value?
- What are your priorities for the year? What are your primary goals for this year?

- What do you want your culture to create?
- What outcomes is your current culture producing?

- How does your current strategy match the culture of the organization?
  - In what ways is your culture fully aligned with your strategy?
  - In what ways does the culture need to change?

- If you could change one to three things about your current culture, what would you change?
  - If you could affect this change, how would the culture be different?

- What are your greatest fears relative to your organization? What are you most concerned about?
  - How fearful is your culture?
  - What creates fear in your culture?

- How optimistic is your culture about the future of the organization and its members?
  - What creates that optimism?

- How does your culture create an emotional connection with the people? How does it help the organization become an entity that people really want to be a part of and that compels people to create exceptional outcomes?

Connecting Points: Be interested in how your people experience the culture, the feelings they have about the changes that are occurring, and what <u>they</u> would like to see change.

Ask top performers:

- What are your goals for the year? What would you say your personal objectives are?
  - Whose help do you need to achieve them?

- What do you think is changing the most around here? How do you see that change?

- What would you like to change about your team or work or the organization?
  - Whose help would you need to make some of those changes?

CONFIDENCE IN LEADERSHIP

Knowing the expected outcomes is a hallmark of engagement and symptomatic of the most productive MicroCultures, yet organization members are often starved for more in the way of direction and purpose. This direction ideally comes from leadership. The confidence in leaders is one of the variables we know transcends local and MacroCulture; this factor is influenced by the immediate supervisor but must be reinforced by leadership. Leadership confidence is a reflection of what leaders say and what they do and from the confidence their leaders express in them.

Leaders intend certain things by their communications, but members must infer from their actions. Often the inferences do not match the intentions.

Ask yourself:

- How confident is the organization with our leadership?
    - What are they confident about?
- What inspires our best players? In what do they trust?
- How do our customers describe our vision?
    - How do they describe our partnership?
- What impact do we have on their business? As leaders, what issues do we hear the most about? The least about?

Connecting Points: Be interested in how people see your role and the issues and concerns they confide in you.

Ask top performers:

- If you were me, what would you pay attention to right now?
- What suggestions do you have for me or the team that could improve our effectiveness or the way we work together?

LINE-OF-SIGHT

There can be no meaningful line-of-sight when senior leadership is cloistered away, reviewing sanitized versions of reality from the people they depend upon to keep things predictable. Sadly, much of leadership's intelligence about customers comes devoid of the emotional connection that makes it meaningful.

Line-of-sight must play out through leaders' actions, day in and day out. Think *customer or die*. Think partner up or waste your fruits on the vine. It is in service to others that we discover the greatest satisfactions in our lives.

When you cannot find yourself renewed and exhilarated when your partners or customers succeed beyond expectations, you have the wrong customers and partners in your life.

Ask yourself:

- What emotional connections does our brand strategy depend upon?
    - What connects our customer to our product/service?
    - How do we assess the strength of that emotional connection?
- What are the inherent risks/dangers to the organization or its culture?
- What decisions are being made as close to the action as possible?

At the grassroots level, your employees/associates often feel more connected to their customers than to their leaders and managers. Employees can begin to think, "They (leaders) don't understand us (customers and employees)." Once that belief takes root, the opposition (passive and active) to leadership-initiated change increases.

Connecting Points: Be interested in the experiences your people have with your customers; ask them to share their stories with you.

Ask top performers:

- What are you learning from our customers? What are their goals?
- From your perspective, what could we do better—or more of?
    - What should we quit doing—or do less of?
- What decisions are you not permitted to make that you should be making?

ENERGY AND ENGAGEMENT

Most organizational cultures misuse the energy of their people. It's a national tragedy that we fail to engage more than half of our workforce, turning potential productive energy into a waste of time and talent while draining our people's cells of their inherent (natural) ability to recharge. We return associates to their homes at the end of the day angry, spent, and disillusioned with their own ability to affect their world in meaningful ways.

The state of energy and engagement is a barometer to the viability of culture.

Ask yourself:

- What is our associate profile (i.e., percent Actively Engaged, Passengers, or Actively Dis-engaged)?
- What level of human energy are we really employing versus misusing, day to day?
- When we rethink engagement from the standpoint of energy, what percentage of our energy is being misdirected or wasted?
- What is the state of innovation within?
    - What new discoveries and spontaneous eruptions of creativity have emerged over the past twelve months?
- In our communications, what do we ask our people versus what we tell them?
- What are people electing to improve? Yearning to learn?
    - Relative to our people's development, what do we encourage them to choose versus what we prescribe?
- What measures are we currently employing to assess the level of relationship, cooperation, and connectedness within our organization?

Connecting Points: Be interested in how people feel when they leave work every day. Find out how satisfied they are with their accomplishments.

Ask top performers:

- What energizes you at work? What motivates and encourages you?
- What are the things that drain energy from you, that you wish could be minimized or eliminated?

MANAGERS

There is no substitute for great management at the local level. No matter what other structures and supports are in place, the manager (or immediate supervisor) is key to individual engagement. For the managers who report to the executive level, this is equally important; the leader must provide the support, connection, and relationship for the managers who report to her.

When considering the strength and impact of management and leadership, every leader must begin with his or her own team (direct reports).

Ask yourself:

- Who's in your circle? Identify the people whose counsel and support you rely upon most.
    - If this is the "In circle" who is in the "Out circle?" (Whose counsel do you avoid or ignore?)
- How many objections or contradictory ideas do you hear day to day? (Are all your ideas brilliant? Are your jokes always funny?)
    - Who can you count on to "set you straight"?
    - Ask this question of those you manage: Whose counsel do you seek?
- How does your organization identify future managers and leaders?
    - How involved are you in that process?
    - How successful has it proven (how many new leaders and managers consistently exceed your expectations)?
- As an individual leader or manager, who, specifically, are you coaching or mentoring?
    - What are that person's talents?
    - What do you expect from him or her?
- How strong is your bench (who could replace you)?
    - Ask your team this question: How strong is your bench?
    - What kind of leverage does this yield for the organization?

Connecting Points: Be interested in the relationships your people have with their manager and the manager's ability to recognize specific talents and successes of the people on his or her team.

Ask top performers:

- If you could clone anyone on your team, who would it be? What are the qualities or talents that person brings to work?
- What are that person's short-term goals? What are they looking to take on or do next?
- In your view, what are some of the ways to maximize this person's growth or performance? Are there some roles or activities they could really benefit from?
- Could this person replace you if you took on other responsibilities? What would they need to do to meet that challenge?

TALENT

People are the culture. It can't exist without them and continuously reflects them. The human condition is messy, but it remains the single most critical element in achieving sustainable growth. Thus, the people who join and those who stay make or break the organization's goals. The more talented the people, the greater the capacity for change and growth.

Our front line is often our most vulnerable line, comprised of people with the least amount of experience, education, and training. Frequently they are regarded as mere butts in seats—interchangeable pegs we force into our square organizational holes.

The state of your talent is the state of your culture.

Ask yourself:

- What are the similarities or differences between the long-term members of this organization and the people who have joined more recently?
- What are the tickets to admission in your organization?
  - What talents/strengths must people bring with them to fit your culture, strategy, and goals?
  - What talents do you most need to grow?
  - What necessary capabilities are in short evidence but critical to your culture and/or strategy?
- What process is in place to insure each new hire raises the bar on the talent within the organization?

- How do we know?
- How do we know when a new hire is a poor fit?
  - How soon do we know?
  - Are we rehiring the best new players, or are we just tolerating those we have selected?
- Does your culture laugh with people or at them?

Connecting Points: Be interested in your supervisors' and managers' appreciation for talent; the immediate supervisor or manager is key to maximizing the talent of the organization, but these efforts are heavily dependent upon the incumbents.

Ask top performers:

- What does your team do better than 97 percent of other teams in the company?
  - What does this tell you about the local culture you've created?

BRIDGECULTURE

Fractures in the BridgeCulture result in enormous energy drains within the organization. Chasms form in the absence of relationship and clear line-of-sight to the real outcomes. Traditionally, organizations have attempted to heal the fractures with transactional data. Unfortunately, this often pulls the groups further apart as the nature of the concerns are more emotional than rational.

Highly productive BridgeCultures are spontaneous engines for innovation through partnership and shared line-of-sight. Breaking out of the confines of structure and due process to create efficient, more impactful solutions requires that the department/groups see themselves (and the BridgeCulture they share) differently. The cultural inquiry should reflect that—and lead to this desired state.

Start with specific departments or work-unit connections critical to your business; where are the opportunities for excellence? For example, between marketing and sales, sales and distribution, or manufacturing and procurement?

Ask yourself:

- Where are our most valuable hand-off connections occurring?
  - What are the critical outcomes of that connection? (What really matters?)
  - How do we measure the quality of the hand-off?
- How do our most critical business imperatives cross organizational boundaries?

BridgeCulture is so critical to organizations that we often need to create a new process and conversation between key departments to help each side better describe its needs and translate the working relationship from inputs and outputs to partnership and line-of sight.

To support that notion, we encourage reciprocal insights, enabling departments or work units to see themselves from the partner's viewpoint. This creates a mirror-like effect because each group can see both their own view as well as their partner's view regarding the same items. This dialogue stimulates better understanding of the partnership's end result and keeps the focus off the transactional items, which can become like white noise.

When people have a strong, trusting partnership with one another, they can turn their attention to mutual outcomes, shared goals, and line-of-sight with the customer.

Connecting Points: Be interested in the relationships among your critically connected departments and the people within them. Do the people within the organization play as if they are all on the same team, keeping score on the right outcomes?

Ask top performers:

- What does Department A do that helps you most, Department B?
  - How do they help you operate at your very best? Feel like a valued partner?
  - What do they do that helps you effectively respond to your customer's needs?
  - If there were one, two, or three things that you could change about this hand-off, what would they be?
- What does Department A need from you to be effective?
  - How do you know?

- - With whom do you work most closely?
- Tell me about a recent success you've had.
  - How did Department A really anticipate what you would need and then provide it?
- Tell me about the feedback you've received from Department B. What are some of the recommendations coming to your team from that group?
  - What are some of the recommendations you have provided to that group?
- Of all the groups (departments or divisions) in the organization, which are the most service-oriented? What are they doing that makes a difference in your working relationship?

MEASUREMENT: THE DEVIL IN THE DETAILS

Challenge the status quo. If it survives the challenge, keep it. Poor measurement destroys energy; the right measurement motivates the team.

Ask yourself:

- What are the most significant outcomes for your organization?
  - How can each person tie his or her performance to at least one of these outcomes?
- What are the implications for the way you are measuring the organization's culture of growth?

Move beyond transactional measures and focus on the development of customer loyalty. Eliminate transactional internal customer service scores and focus on creating a phenomenal breakout BridgeCulture.

- How do you measure the interdepartmental synergy?
  - What does it tell you about your overall efficiency and effectiveness?
  - Where is energy wasted on dysfunctional systems or processes?

Relationship must be measured at the nuclear level because one of the most important variables in retention and growth is the relationship individuals have with their managers. Finding the right measurement is critical to insuring that every team has the leadership they need to maximize the gifts of its members.

- How do we determine the range of energy within our nuclear cultures?
- Where are we wasting the energy we employ?

We talk growth but rarely take the time to understand what real growth looks like. Faux growth has us chasing our tails and sapping our energy and commitment. Keep a sharp focus on the growth that matters; it's a one-two punch: (1) Sales growth first and foremost, which creates opportunity for (2) People growing to meet new challenges.

Healthy MicroCultures are incubators for individual growth. And if the people aren't individually growing, the organizational progress may be nearing its peak.

- Which high-potential players could you mentor or coach?
- What people are currently being coached or mentored by other leaders in the organization?

Connecting Points: Be interested in the way your people assess performance relative to the critical outcomes of your business. This means focusing on both rational (financial, performance, market share) and emotional (customer loyalty and employee engagement) outcomes.

Ask top performers:

- What's your experience with the performance appraisal process we currently have in place?
  - Do your people (or do you) agree about your performance as indicated by that process?
- What data/metrics do we currently collect that are not useful to you?
- What should we collect that we don't have?

ENDNOTES

[1] 32 percent of employees are operating at less than 40 percent of capacity. Coffman Research Institute, 2013, Vol 6: 3.

[2] http://www.govexec.com/excellence/promising-practices/2013/03/4-reasons-why-investing-employee-engagement-matters/62098/.

[3] http://www.dalecarnegie.com/imap/white_papers/employee_engagement_white_paper/

[4] http://leaderchat.org/2011/09/01/poor-leadership-costs-average-organization-over-1-million-dollars-annually/

[5] http://hbr.org/2011/09/why-your-it-project-may-be-riskier-than-you-think/

[6] Muggsy Bogues was five foot three inches tall and 136 pounds in his playing days.

[7] Oakland Raiders website, http://www.Raiders.com.

[8] Raider Haters website, http://www.chargertom.com/RaiderHaters.html.

[9] Bill Clinton, *My Life* (New York: Knopf, 2004), 45.

[10] "National University Rankings," *US News and World Report*, http://colleges.usnews.rankingsandreviews.com/best-colleges/rankings/national-universities/data#.

[11] Studies have revealed the importance of a best friend at work or the satisfaction employees feel when they can say, "One of my best friends is also my colleague" and the pride employees feel in the statement, "My manager seems to care about me." These items (survey questions) and dozens of others like them are used throughout the world to capture the essence of the importance of relationships at work.

[12] http://www.adcouncil.org/Our-Work/The-Classics/United-Negro-College-Fund

[13] Marcus Buckingham and Curt Coffman, *First, Break All the Rules: What the World's Greatest Managers Do Differently* (New York: Simon and Schuster, 1999), pg. 200.

[14] In the process of writing this, we attempted some due diligence with respect to Johnny's title, researching his designation on the World Wide Web. While we were unable to find definitive proof of his legendary status, the point is that *he knows* it to be true. Other references to the "world's best bus driver" revealed this designation referred strictly to driving prowess. Finally, the sheer volume of references to drivers who were rude, spit on passengers, beat them up, and even ran them over is certainly a tangible reminder that we find at least ten negatives to every positive.

[15] Most Interesting Man in the World videos, Dos Equis website, http://dosequis.com.

[16] The CBS sitcom enjoyed years of success and killer Nielsen ratings. At the time of this publication, Ashton Kutcher has been placed in the enviable position of resurrecting the franchise.

[17] Engagement research links the person's ability to use his or her talents to employee retention, margin, and customer engagement.

[18] Coffman Research Institute, 2011, Vol 5:2.

[19] "He who shall not be named" refers to the villainous Lord Voldemort in *Harry Potter and the Sorcerer's Stone* and its sequels by J. K. Rowling.

[20] *The Secret* by Rhonda Byrne is a worldwide bestseller now published in over forty-seven languages.

[21] *The Emperor's New Clothes* is the fable about an arrogant emperor who was duped by an enterprising con man into thinking that only "worthy" individuals could see the fine-spun clothing the con man sold the emperor. The emperor himself and his constituency were all forced into pretending they could see the invisible garments until a young boy broke the spell: "But he's not wearing anything at all." We sometimes observe cultures conspiring to see leaders where few are truly given the space to lead.

[22] *All I Really Need to Know I Learned in Kindergarten*, the book by Robert Fulghum, has a great deal of fun with this notion.

[23] Realtor is the trademark of an organization of licensed real estate professionals.

[24] For Sale by Owner here refers to homes sold without the services of a real estate professional and not the FSBO trademarked organization.

[25] "Walmarting" refers to Walmart's cost-cutting practices, which have resulted in its tremendous success as a retailer whose strategy clearly aligns with its culture. Yet organizations that seek to adopt this strategy should be cautioned to verify that their own businesses are prepared to become commodities in the mind of their customers.

[26] Richard Conniff, *The Ape in the Corner Office: Understanding the Workplace Beast in All of Us* (New York: Crown Business, 2005), 91.

[27] Chris Meadows, "Lessons from Circuit City's Bankruptcy," *TeleRead*, http://www.teleread.com/drm/lessons-from-circuit-citys-bankruptcy/.

[28] www.michelin.com/corporate/group/history.

[29] William J. Bennett, "US Lag in Science, Math a Disaster in the Making," CNN, http://www.cnn.com/2012/02/09/opinion/bennett-stem-education/index.html.

[30] Gugler K. Mueller D.C., Yurtoglu B.B. and Zulehner C. (2003). The effects of mergers: an international comparison. International Journal of Industrial Organization 21, 625-653.

[31] The Family Council Handbook: How to Create, Run, and Maintain a Successful Family Business Council (Macmillan 2012) By Christopher J. Eckrich, Stephen L. McClure

[32] Kramer, Robert. "The Birth of Client-Centered Therapy : Carl Rogers, Otto Rank, and 'The Beyond'". *Journal of Humanistic Psychology*, 35.4 (1995) p. 54-110.

[33] Coffman Research Institute, 2012, Vol 4:5.

[34] Coffman Research Institute, 2012, Vol 4:7.

[35] Coffman Research Institute, 2012, Vol 4:7.

[36] "The Danger of Laughing at Your Customers," *37Signals* (blog), http://37signals.com/svn/posts/1216-the-danger-of-laughing-at-your-customers.

[37] http://www.fedprimerate.com/dow-jones-industrial-average-history-djia.htm

[38] Neil F. Neimark, MD, "The Fight or Flight Response," The Body/Soul Connection, http://www.thebodysoulconnection.com/EducationCenter/fight.html.

[39] Coffman Research Institute, 2009, Vol 3:2.

[40] Coffman Research Institute, 2013, Vol 5:3.

[41] Ricky Gervais is the award-winning creator and star of the original BBC series *The Office* and HBO's *Extras*. *The Invention of Lying*, Warner Home Video, 2009.

[42] Reference to Jack Nicholson's famous character, Colonel Jessup, in the movie *A Few Good Men*. Nicholson (as Jessup) explains that a cover-up was necessary because others (civilians, the staffers, and weak leaders) couldn't handle the truth.

[43] Coffman Research Insitute, 2012. Vol 6:2.

[44] Tony Horton infomercial – Beach Bodies. http://www.beachbody.com/product/how-p90x-works-muscle-confusion.do.

[45] This story, told by a consultant friend, Larry, who was watching Hogan himself when he heard the fan's question and Hogan's response.

[46] A relatively recent Travelers Insurance commercial shows a sleepless dog worrying relentlessly about his bone (burying it, digging it up, and banking it) until it finally rests it under the protective Travelers umbrella. "Worry, worry, worry" the song refrains as the dog cannot sleep due to his concern for the bone. Perhaps worry is an odd term, but we use it here because work orientation is one of the most predominant of the talent sets of outstanding performers in any role. It is rare to find a great leader, manager, or associate who does not continuously think about, review, and rehearse his or her work.

[47] Coffman Research Institute, 2013, Vol 5:4.

[48] http://www.golf.com/tour-and-news/rory-mcilroy-19-has-game-and-charisma-

CESFL ACKNOWLEDGMENTS

To say this book was written "by Kathie and Curt" would be misleading. Without the significant contributions made by so many people, this book would never have reached the printer's press.

Topping that list are the millions of employees, managers, leaders and clients who have shown us exactly what excellence looks like relative to culture. Thank you! You have defined the standard that will help insure every person has a great place to work. Success is unavoidable when the people are given a voice.

Our colleague, Geoff Willcox is the steady influence behind our interviews, data organization and analysis. He is committed to relentlessly translating the data into meaningful use. Without Geoff's contribution, this book would be missing its heart.

Peg Breen played such a critical role in setting the course for this book and nudging it until momentum took over.

These business partners have helped us keep our cause clear; they have been a blessing in many different ways: Anil Saxena, Eric Sandberg, Ethan Bondelid, Jared Rathe, Michelle Wallace, Robert Bond, Rod Benson, and Ron Snell.

Our research, like most business, is global and therefore would not have been possible without our incredibly smart, international associates at PeopleBusiness-Coffman: Akhilesh Mandal, Ashish Ambasta, Barath Jain, Georgie Antony, Mervyn Raphael, Michael Fernandes, Naveen Kumar, Rohit Shenoy, Sarojani Gaikwad, Saurabh Gahrota, Soumaditya Mukherjee.

Discoveries require a prepared mind and gratefully, we have worked side-by-side with some of the most notable thought leaders of our time. Adam Roth, AJ Scribante, Alan Scott, Alec Gallup, Benson Smith, Beverly Kaye, Bob Donegan, Bob Nielsen, Brandon Curry, Bret Pawlowski, Dr. Bruce Avolio, Dr. Deb Manning, Dr. Don Clifton, Dr. Frank Byrne, Dr. Fred Luthans, George Borst, George Gallup, Jim Collins, Dr. Jim Harter, Dr. Jim Sorensen, John Timmerman, Marcus Buckingham, Dr. Mick Zangari, Dr. Mike Morrison, Dr. Paul Welter, Dr. Richard Abrams, Dr. Stephen Haag, Steve King, and Dr. Ted Hayes. Your relationships and encouragement have shaped who we are and the discoveries we have made.

We want to call out our supporters & friends who keep our passion moving forward: Alan, Ben, Betty, Bob, Bobby, Brady, Brandi Jo, Brandon, Brett,